Devotion to St. Joseph: Read-Aloud Stories, Poems, and Prayers for Catholic Children

Stories by
Sr. Margaret Patrice
Wilfrid Sheed
Catherine Beebe
Sr. Mary Charitas
Mary Mannix

Compiled, Edited, and Supplemented by
Janet P. McKenzie, OCDS

Biblio Resource Publications, Inc.
Bessemer, MI 49911
2011

© 2011 by Janet P. McKenzie

All right reserved. No part of this book may be reproduced, stored in a retrieval system, or transmitted, in any form or by any means, electronic, mechanical, photocopying, recording, or otherwise, without the written permission of the author.

ISBN 978-1-934185-41-4

Published by Biblio Resource Publications, Inc.
108½ South Moore Street, Bessemer, MI 49911
www.BiblioResource.com
info@biblioresource.com

Cover art by Rafaello Busoni

Unless otherwise stated, Scripture texts in this work are taken from the *New American Bible with Revised New Testament* © 1986, 1970 Confraternity of Christian Doctrine, Washington, D.C. and are used by permission of the copyright owner. All Rights Reserved. No part of the *New American Bible* may be reproduced in any form without permission in writing from the copyright owner.

Printed in the United States of America

This book is gratefully dedicated to St. Joseph.

May it inspire many to call upon the help of St. Joseph so that they too may be rewarded by abundant blessings from God.

Table of Contents

Preface .... i-ii

Keeper of the Gate 1-58
    Chapter One 3-12
    Chapter Two 13-20
    Chapter Three 21-26
    Chapter Four 27-36
    Chapter Five 37-42
    Chapter Six 43-50
    Chapter Seven 51-58

St. Joseph: The Hidden Saint Who Served God 59-64

St. Joseph: Patron of the Universal Church 65-72

The Man Who Built the Secret Door 73-84

St. Joseph: Powerful Intercessor 85-94

Poems about St. Joseph 95-101

Prayers to St. Joseph 103-108

Acknowledgements 109-110

More RACE for Heaven Products 111-119

Preface

St. Joseph was chosen by God to care for and protect the Savior of the world and His mother—to be head of the Holy Family. Yet Scripture does not record a single word this great saint spoke; we must take our lessons of his life from his actions. In this compilation of stories and poems about our Savior's foster-father, we are encouraged to imitate the virtues the life of St. Joseph reveal to us in his loving dedication to Jesus and Mary.

By reading inspiring stories and poems by renowned children's authors and poets, young Catholics are sure to acquire a greater understanding of—and devotion to—the earthly father of Jesus. The discussion questions as well as the reflections on the virtues of St. Joseph lead children to apply the lessons of this saint's life to their own. The concluding section of this book contains prayers to St. Joseph, a short litany for children, prayers for the Nine First Wednesdays of St. Joseph, and an Act of Consecration to St. Joseph.

Perhaps no one can promote a devotion to St. Joseph as eloquently and convincingly as St. Teresa of Avila, who had a rich and long-running relationship with him. In her autobiography, *The Book of Her Life*, Chapter 6, she tells us:

> I took for my advocate and lord the glorious Saint Joseph and commended myself earnestly to him; and I found . . . that he gave me greater blessings than I could ask of him. I do not remember even now that I have ever asked anything of him which he has failed to grant. I am astonished at the great favors which God has bestowed on me through this

blessed saint, and at the perils from which He has freed me, both in body and in soul. To other saints the Lord seems to have given grace to help us in some of our necessities but of this glorious saint my experience is that he helps us in them all and that the Lord wishes to teach us that as He was Himself subject to him on earth, just so in heaven He still does all that [St. Joseph] asks.

. . . I wish I could persuade everyone to be devoted to this glorious saint, for I have great experience of the blessings which he can obtain from God. I have never known anyone to be truly devoted to him and render him particular services who did not notably advance in virtue, for he gives very real help to souls who commend themselves to him. For some years now, I think, I have made some request of him every year on his festival and I have always had it granted. If my petition is in any way ill directed, he directs it aright for my greater good.

. . . If anyone cannot find a master to teach him how to pray, let him take this glorious saint as his master and he will not go astray.

If we remember that Teresa of Avila, the great Carmelite reformer, become not only a saint but a Doctor of the Church as well, we must place great confidence in her words and recommendations. Let us learn from St. Teresa of Avila to honor and imitate St. Joseph and, through this saintly devotion, see what favors God bestows upon us!

Janet P. McKenzie, OCDS
October 5, 2011
Feast of St. Faustina Kowalska

Keeper of the Gate

Sister Margaret Patrice

Chapter One
Keeper of the Gate

EVERYONE likes a true story. This story is not only true, it is full of adventure. What is adventure? It is a going out into the unknown without fear. A soldier is an adventurer when he charges the enemy. So, too, is a fireman when he enters a flaming building, a doctor when he fights disease, a football player when he dashes into the line. These men have strong and daring hearts. They do not hesitate once they are aroused to duty; they go straight to the mark without fear.

The brave man in this story is St. Joseph of Nazareth, in Palestine, a little country no bigger than Switzerland or New Hampshire. Although he lived over nineteen hundred years ago, he is still one of the most talked-of men in the world. Names of places like Bethlehem and Galilee connected with his life are holy words known in all corners of the world by people who may never have heard of Paris or Chicago.

Joseph was a blue blood. He had a long family tree. He belonged to the royal line of David, the greatest of all the kings of Israel. Joseph could count princes, prophets, and patriarchs among his ancestors. He might have been a king himself if the throne of David had not been taken from his family line. Yet, he did not care whether he was king or not. He was very sensible about it. He would not bribe himself into high office. He liked to work. It gave him a feeling of self-respect. Moreover, in his time, wealth did not count so very much with the Jews. Every boy learned a trade regardless of whether he was rich or poor. You will remember that St. Paul was a tentmaker, Matthew, a tax collector, John, a fisherman, Simon, a tanner, Thomas, a master builder. Joseph had a trade, too. He was a carpenter.

Joseph liked to work. It gave him a feeling of self-respect.

Keeper of the Gate

The New Testament tells us very little about St. Joseph. But he must have been a very extraordinary man since God chose him to be the guardian of Jesus and the protector of Mary. There is a very beautiful legend that shows what God thought of Joseph. Our Blessed Lady, at this time, was a young girl. She had been in the service of the Temple from the time she was three years old. The Temple was the most important church of the Jews. It was a Jewish custom for girls to consecrate long years of devotion to its service. Here they learned to make the incense for the morning and evening prayer offerings, to bake the holy breads that were laid in gold-covered tables, to embroider with gold and silver threads, and other useful tasks.

It was now time for Mary to marry. Zachary, the high priest, spoke to his council about choosing a husband for her. "Men, Brethren," he said, "Mary is a pattern for our daughters. She does all things well, has great skill, is good to the poor; she should be married to one great and honorable, one most excellent in virtue." The council agreed to this. So they searched the records and genealogies in order to select the noblest man in all Israel.

Many suitable men were notified to come to the Temple. Some were wealthy and handsome, many of them held a high rank in Jerusalem. Among them was Joseph. Each man carried a staff, as was the custom among Jews. When Zachary saw so many eligible men he was at a loss to know which to choose. "God of my fathers, inspire me! Give me a sign by which the right man will be known to me," he prayed. Turning to the young men, he said: "Brethren, Mary surpasses all maidens in sweetness and virtue. She is of royal worth in all ways. It is hard to choose one from among you; so let each of you write his name upon his staff, leave it in the sanctuary, and return in the morning for my answer."

The men were disappointed. However, they had not long to wait. Early the next morning, they went with Zachary to the sanctuary. When the door was opened, a burst of exquisite fragrance filled the air. Looking in, Zachary saw the most beautiful lilies that he had ever seen blooming on one of the rods. It was Joseph's rod. All the other rods remained as they had been the night before. While Joseph's friends anointed him, the disappointed suitors bowed to Joseph and broke their rods. The date was then set for the wedding.

Marriage customs in the East differed from those of our country. The espousals were the same as our engagement, except that a Jewish "engagement" was legal. It was binding. The real marriage took place much later, at least a year later.

In the meantime, the *almahs*, or women of the Temple, were getting Mary's robe ready for the wedding. It was to be a beautiful amber gown embroidered with silver and gold thread. Mary and Joseph chose their wedding attendants.

On the appointed day trumpets blew long and joyfully, and were heard within the Temple. It was the signal that Joseph and his groomsmen were approaching. The bridesmaids, carrying lighted lamps, came out singing: "Come forth to meet David's dearest daughter." Mary stepped out to the Temple court. Together, she and Joseph mounted other stairs leading to the high priest. Vested in tunic and miter, Zachary was a majestic-looking Jew. The ceremony did not take long. Joseph had brought a ring of purest gold. Zachary put Mary's hand in Joseph's, and the ring was placed on her finger. [This ring may be seen today in Perugia, Italy.] The scribe recorded the marriage and the nuptial song was sung.

*Zachary put Mary's hand in Joseph's and
the ring was placed on her finger.*

Down to Nazareth Joseph took Mary. "Nazareth" means "flower," and Joseph rejoiced that he had the fairest flower in all Israel, Mary. The house he had built for her was a small, lime-white, cozy little home that nestled among pine-scented hills. The sun streamed in golden rays upon the purple grapes in the arbor behind the house.

Devotion to St. Joseph

As the bridal couple approached their home for the marriage feast, they saw that many of the wedding guests had already assembled on the terraced hillock. Flute players and harpists filled the air with exquisite music. In the women's section of the house the girls danced and made merry with the young bride. The men, of course, talked about crops and taxes, just as men do today.

Finally, the feasting came to an end. The last guest had gone. Joseph and Mary were alone. Like all brides, Mary talked about the wedding again and again—who their guests had been, and remarked that she did not deserve the lovely gifts they had given her. There was a distaff covered with flax from Ruth, exquisitely embroidered sandals from Miriam, and beautiful dishes from Ann. These last she decided to keep for best. "Joseph, would you mind if we kept these for special occasions?" she asked. Of course, he would not mind. A cup was a cup to him as it is to most men. Mary was very proud, too, of a handsome dining table that Joseph had made of special unsplintered oak. Many of the guests had noticed it. Three of them left their orders for others just like it.

Joseph began work again. Mary got up early in order to be sure that Joseph had a good breakfast before going out. In fact, she was up before Joseph. She was taking fresh corn bread out of the oven when she heard his heavy sandaled foot in the next room. "M-m-mm, how good that smells, Mary!" he said when he lifted the curtain of the little alcove. Mary knew he liked corn bread.

"You like melons, too. I bought these yesterday," said Mary, pouring fresh goat's milk for two.

After breakfast, Joseph reached for his leather apron that hung behind the door. It was laced with a crimson thong. A kirtle of coarse linen hung below his knees, and he wore sandals of untanned leather. He was tall, strong shouldered, had a deep chest, curly brown hair, and browner eyes. He was a few years older than Mary, which was as it should be. But he was not an old man as Christian art sometimes pictures him.

Joseph's workshop was a little way off, behind the house. What refreshing odors rose from the fragrant pine planks, oak boards, and cedar logs! Let us watch Joseph as he works. He takes off his outer garment so that he can work faster. His arms and neck are bronzed. Large veins stand out in his hands as he uses the saw, the plane, the hammer. He makes and mends cart wheels, plowshares, tables, stools, and chests. His work is well done, although it is rough. His tools are clumsy. Even today carpentry in Nazareth is backward.

He works alone. He cannot pay a helper. He stops from time to time to wipe his brow. At noon he rests. The noonday meal with Mary refreshes him, and the afternoon finds him back at work again. He must take the finished work around to the village homes. His customers like his work. He does not skimp, he uses good materials, he never overcharges. Yet, no matter how low his price he is "beaten down." Sometimes he is not paid for months. "Come back at threshing time," some say. That means he will get wheat or barley grain for payment, or, perhaps, it will be olives or wool.

One day, soon after their marriage, Mary said to Joseph, "I have not seen my cousin, Elizabeth, for a long time. She is quite old now, and she may not be well. I think I will go to see her." We do not know whether Joseph went with Mary on this journey or not; most likely, he escorted her both ways. It was at least eighty miles from Nazareth to Judea. He would never let her go alone that distance.

Elizabeth was delighted to see Mary. Three months Mary stayed with her cousin. Joseph missed her a great deal. The house was lonely, and he had to get his own meals.

But, when Mary was back again in Nazareth, Joseph was happy. Once more Mary and he enjoyed the quiet evenings after work. They sat on the flat roof of their little home and chatted. Sometimes it was Mary who talked. She liked to tell over and over again about Elizabeth's wonderful little baby, John. She liked to tell about the unusual events connected with his birth.

At other times it would be Joseph who did the talking. He was a Jew, and like other descendants of David, he believed in the coming of the Messiah. He enjoyed talking about it, and what a wonderful thing it would be for the Jews. There were some nights when neither Joseph nor Mary seemed to have much to say. Each of them wanted to talk, each seemed to have a secret he and she wanted the other to know, but neither could begin.

Yet, nobody could say that Mary was not happy. She sang more now than ever. One evening, as she was doing the supper dishes, Joseph said, "Mary, you have been singing snatches of some new hymns since you came home from Elizabeth's house. I like them. Come out on the porch and sing them for me."

"I am so glad you like them, Joseph," said Mary, as they went out to the leafy bower behind the house. "One of them is the *Benedictus*, the song that Zachary sang in thanksgiving to God for the new baby, John. The other is my own, Joseph."

They stood beside an almond tree in full pink bloom facing Jerusalem and the Temple. A new moon threw a silver sheen on Mary's blue mantle. Softly and sweetly she sang her *Magnificat:*

"My soul proclaims the greatness of the Lord,
My spirit rejoices in God my Savior for he has
looked with favor on his lowly servant.
From this day all generations will call me blessed:
The Almighty has done great things for me, and
holy is his Name.
He has mercy on those who fear him in every
generation.
He has shown the strength of his arm;
he has scattered the proud in their conceit.
He has cast down the mighty from their thrones,
and has lifted up the lowly.
He has filled the hungry with good things,
and the rich he has sent away empty.
He has come to the help of his servant Israel for he
has remembered his promise of mercy,
the promise he made to our fathers,
to Abraham and his children forever."[1]

When she finished Joseph said, "Mary, you sing sweetly; that is a beautiful hymn; you are like a queen. You are Heaven's Queen." Mary looked at him in sweet wonder, and thought, "Does he know what the Angel Gabriel told me? God does, sometimes, tell His secrets to His special friends."

Joseph seemed to guess Mary's thoughts. "Yes, dear, I understand," he said. "An angel told me."

"'An angel' . . . well, that was not so strange. God often sent His angels as messengers to men. It was nothing new to the Jews to have angels appear to them. An angel was promised to Moses; then there were Tobit and Joshua," thought Mary.

---

[1] See Luke 1:46-55.

The night air was getting quite chilly, so Joseph drew Mary's mantle closer about her shoulders, saying at the same time, "Mary, you are the very Gate of Heaven,[2] dear."

"Well, Joseph, you take such good care of me," said Mary, "I shall have to call you *the Keeper of the Gate.*"

Discussion Questions
1. What can we learn about the proper attitude of work from St. Joseph?
2. What can we learn about the virtue of love from St. Joseph?
3. Explain Joseph's title as "Keeper of the Gate."

Virtues of St. Joseph
In all things, no matter what the circumstances, we see St. Joseph as being always open to whatever plan God has in mind for him. He listens with his whole heart to what God tells him. He accepts what God says without consulting or sharing with others. How can you imitate the quiet obedience and acceptance of St. Joseph?

---

[2] Title of Mary as honored in the Litany of the Blessed Virgin Mary (Litany of Loretto)

Chapter Two
Christmas Joy

JOSEPH and Mary were very happy in their Nazareth home. They looked forward to spending all their lives there. Joseph was well thought of in the village. He was a just man. That means he was fair in all his dealings with others. He was a respectable craftsman. He was proud of their little home. He had built it; it was theirs. Mary was a good housekeeper. "None better," Joseph would say, "her bread is simply delicious. The crust would melt in your mouth, golden and crisp, baked three times a week."

One evening, after supper, Joseph and Mary were chatting. He was whittling a spoon and Mary was sewing. A knock at the door! Mary opened it. "Ave, ave, friends," said old Benjamin and his brother, Esau. "Have you heard the news?"

Without waiting for Joseph's reply, Esau said, "The village is all posted up with announcements from the emperor. He is after taxes again."

"Every Jew must go to his place of birth to be enrolled. I tell you Rome flaunts her banners on our hills now, but the day will come when Caesar will be humbled. The Lord God of Israel will come, the mighty Son of David. The King of Israel will come. He will be our King. He will be born in splendor. He shall rule, and haughty Rome will tremble!" vowed the old man.

"This enrollment, or census taking, is going to be quite an inconvenience," said Joseph, "but let us be of good cheer, friends. In God's sight there is no difference between the rich and the poor, between the highborn and the low. When men are more like God, they will have love for each other." Mary looked troubled, but Joseph laid his hand on her shoulder and told her not to worry.

While they were talking, a trumpet blast blew loud and shrill. From the door they could see a mounted camel rider padding up the hill with a troop of children behind him. It was no ordinary-looking camel. This one had a jeweled harness and silver trappings. His rider shouted his message like a town crier. "Vah! Vah! get along out of here, you scheming old Roman," muttered Esau under his breath. Jews had no use for Romans. It was only about forty years before Joseph was born that one of them had captured Jerusalem.

Benjamin too had his ideas about this affair. "You see, friends," he said, "the emperor, certainly, has not thought of what this might mean to poor people. This is no time of the year to travel. It means losing time from work, too."

Joseph was saddened, not for himself, but for Mary. How would she stand such a long trip? However, Mary loved Joseph. She would go where he went. So she lost no time getting ready for the trip. "You had better wear your winter sandals, Mary," suggested Joseph, "those with the hempen thread; they are warmer." Carefully, Mary placed her unfinished sewing in the cedar chest. That afternoon she had brought an extra jug of water from the well. She had planned to wash in the morning. "I should do it now, if we expect to get an early start," she said to Joseph.

"Yes, and I shall plane that stool for Miriam. I can deliver it on the way down tomorrow."

The next morning, while Joseph fed Donkey Oaty, Mary wrapped up some bread, figs, and a measure of olive oil. They closed the house and stuck the bolt in the door. Joseph spread a blanket over the saddle for Mary, took his staff, and off they went. They were not especially happy about going on this trip. It would be a five-day journey to Bethlehem. That was Joseph's town because it had been King David's town. The roads were rough. Other families went past them on camels. Joseph saluted them in a friendly way. Sometimes, they met other relatives when they stopped at the wells. Gradually, they went farther and deeper into the Judean hills, fewer and fewer caravans passed, and it grew more and more lonely.

After five days' travel, they reached Bethlehem, late at night, exhausted and hungry. Even Donkey Oaty was so tired he almost rebelled against going another step. How glad they were to see the cheerful glimmer of oil lamps in the distance! The streets were deserted. Everyone had been accommodated before dark. "Even if I could get a small room it would do for tonight, and tomorrow I could, perhaps, find better," thought Joseph. He knocked courteously on one door. The sound of sandals sloshing across the floor seemed to encourage him. "May we come in, my wife and I?" he asked. "We have come a long way. My wife is especially tired."

"I am sorry, sir," the man said, "but we are all filled up with relatives who have come for the enrolling. Try further up."

Further up Joseph went. "Why, can't you see we are entirely filled up?" a cross old innkeeper said to him. Joseph and Mary were refused twice. They would try elsewhere. "Bah!" said the third, grouchy landlord, "You are a poor man. We have rich guests. You cannot pay much. I want a good price for keep here. Go away. Don't bother us!" and the door was rudely shut in Joseph's face.

Mary tried to cheer Joseph. "Look, there's a jolly group

in there," she said pointing at a half-opened door. "There are several women in there, too. Surely they will have a little pity on us." In answer to Joseph's knock the innkeeper's wife came to the door. Just as she was about to say "Come in," her husband, who had seen through the door and heard the conversation, called to her: "Come, wife, why keep the wine waiting? Our guests call for it."

"Bah! You are a poor man. Go away.
Don't bother us!"

Again Joseph was refused. So many doors were closed on this holy pair. They tried all over town for a room, and none could be found.

This was especially hard for Joseph. Here he was begging for a room when he would gladly have worked his fingers off to pay any price for one. When he looked at Mary's sweet, tired face, he was grieved to think that she would possibly have to spend the night out on the open hillsides.

One by one the lights in Bethlehem went out, the noise and laughter ceased, and the people settled down for the night. The streets were dark and unfriendly. However, the moon was kind to them. It shed a bright, protecting halo around them. Joseph knelt and prayed for a minute for direction. Off in the distance the moon showed the outline of a cave such as is used for sheep when storms arise during the night. "We shall go over there," he said to Mary. "It is not a very nice place to spend the night, but it is the best we can do. At least we can sit and rest in quiet."

When they reached the cave, they paused for a moment at the entrance. A few stray moonbeams played about on the dusty floor. Br-r-r, it was chilly! December on the Judean hills was always cold. Over in one corner of the cave were the remains of the last fire that shepherds had left there. Joseph tied Donkey Oaty in the corner, swept up the old ashes, and laid sticks for a new fire. Mary divided their little supper. "There is a little milk in the goatskin. I will heat it for you, Mary. I'll get a light from some shepherds on the other side of the hill. We passed them on the way down. I won't be long gone, dear."

Mary did not see the tears in his eyes. He was glad that she had not noticed. How it pained him to think of her. "Well, it cannot be helped," he thought. He was not a man to sit down and whine about things. He was a man of action. He always did something. "This is the way God has arranged things, and God makes no mistakes," he said half aloud.

Quite a distance over, on the other side of the hill, shepherds were tending their flocks. They were huddled around a little fire they had made. It was chilly, and, besides, they needed the red glow of light to scare off wolves that prowled about at night. Imagine the surprise of the shepherds when Joseph approached, asking for a lighted coal, and at that time of night, too! Why, of course, they would give him a light!

Joseph did not stop long to talk. He would not keep Mary waiting; he hurried back, his eyes straining to see the cave in the darkness of the hillside. But what was this? Had Mary kindled a fire? There was a great white and yellow light outside the cave and inside! What could it mean?

Had someone come while he was out? He hurried along, breathless! On the threshold he paused! Mary smiled at him and held up the dear Baby Jesus! Joseph was almost overcome with joy. He was speechless! Instantly he knelt and adored Jesus. How wonderful! Now there were three! Jesus, Mary, and Joseph! They cannot be separated. We never think of one without the others.

Outside, there were voices! A knock! Joseph answered. Shepherds had come. "We were guarding our flocks a mile away when an angel appeared to us, saying, 'Behold! We bring you good news that shall be for all the people; tonight a Savior is born to you who is Christ, the Lord, in Bethlehem.' We have come to adore Him," the shepherds told Joseph.

"Come in," said Joseph. Softly, they stepped over to the manger, dropped on their knees, and adored their new Infant King.

"What are you going to call Him?" asked one of them.

The shepherds dropped to their knees, and adored their new Infant King.

"Jesus," said Joseph, "the name that the angel told me was to be His." Thus it was that St. Joseph was the first to hold Jesus in his arms, was the first to pronounce the name Jesus, and was the first to introduce Jesus to others.

Devotion to St. Joseph

 Discussion Questions

1. What do you think it would be like to ride a donkey (or to walk) in the cold for five days in a row?
2. What did Joseph mean when he said that he would go "get a light" from the shepherds?
3. "He [Joseph] was not a man to sit down and whine about things" (page 17). What are some things about which you complain? What can you do to remind yourself to imitate St. Joseph in this regard?
4. What would it be like to be "the first to hold Jesus . . . the first to pronounce the name Jesus, and . . . the first to introduce Jesus to others" (page 19)?

✝ Virtues of St. Joseph

When Joseph did not know what to do about finding a room for Mary and himself, he "knelt and prayed for a moment for direction" (page 17). In imitation of the faith of St. Joseph, pause to kneel and pray to God the next time you are not sure what would be the best thing to do. Like St. Joseph, try to stop to talk with God often.

Chapter Three
Glad Hearts

SOON after Christmas night, Joseph went up to the office of the censor to register. As he took up the quill, his hand trembled. Nervously, he smoothed out the parchment, dipped the quill, but he could not write his name. "What is the trouble?" asked a scribe who had been watching him.

"Oh, nothing at all," said Joseph. Again he straightened the scroll, stared at it, hesitated, then wrote very hurriedly:

"Joseph, son of Jacob, carpenter"—and his age

"Mary, daughter of Joachim"—and her age

"Jesus, Son of Mary"—and His age.

"That does not seem just right to me," he thought, "my name ahead of Jesus' name. He should have first place." In his humility he had hesitated to put himself first.

Joseph and Mary wanted to go back to Nazareth, but they could not go yet. There was a law among the Jews concerning new babies. Forty days after his birth, the father and mother were obliged to take the new baby up to the Temple, and make a gift offering of a lamb or doves. This was called the Presentation. It went back to the time when God freed the Jews from the yoke of Pharaoh. God told Moses to warn the Egyptians that if they did not free the Jews, whom they had taken into captivity, He would punish them by destroying the oldest son in each Egyptian family.

Pharaoh paid no attention to Moses. Moses then told the Jews to kill a lamb, and sprinkle some of its blood on the outside of their doors. That night the destroying angel entered every house not marked with the blood of the lamb and killed the eldest son in that family. So it was in thanksgiving for having spared the first-born of the Jewish families that Jesus was presented in the Temple. We see now why Jesus is called Mary's "first-born son." In Jewish families even an only son was called the "first-born" because of this law regarding his presentation in the Temple.

Again, Joseph and Mary are traveling. From Bethlehem to Jerusalem it is about five miles. They spent the night outside the city. The next morning Joseph took Jesus and Mary up to the gorgeous Temple with its massive gates, bridges, and stairways. Palestine had many synagogues, but only one Temple. It was a magnificent building, like an immense cathedral on the hill.

Here, again, Mary was depending on Joseph. It was he who brought the five shekels that were offered to the high priest. This sum is only about four dollars in our money, but, to a poor man like Joseph, it was a great deal. It was Joseph who bought the two doves which the mother offered. They could not afford a lamb.

Up the white stone steps of the Temple the holy pair went, up to where the great dome gleamed in the sunlight like snow above the brown walls of the city. Love and joy flooded Joseph's heart as he carried Jesus with him.

In the Temple at the same time was a holy old man called Simeon. He was praying when the Holy Family entered. The minute he looked at the Divine Child he knew Him, and shuffled after Joseph and Mary. Mary was surprised when he stood before them, clasped his hands and said, "Now, Master, you may let your servant go in peace, according to your word, for my eyes have seen your salvation, which you prepared in sight of all the peoples, a light for revelation to the Gentiles, and glory for your people Israel."[3] Our Lady wondered who this man was, and how he knew who this Child was.

Tenderly, she let Simeon hold the Infant. While he pressed Jesus to his heart, he explained to Mary how God had promised him that he would not die until he had seen the Lord. Simeon also told Mary that many people would believe in this Divine Child, and many would not. He prophesied that a great sorrow would one day pierce her heart like a sword.

While they were speaking, Anna, a holy woman, came into the Temple. Mary knew Anna. This was the same Anna who had been in the Temple when Mary lived there. Anna knew who Mary's Child was. From that day on she talked about Him to everyone she met.

All this happened on February second. It was the first Feast of the Purification. It is sometimes called Candlemas Day because, while Simeon held our Blessed Lord, he called Him "a light for revelation to the Gentiles." On this day, the Church blesses the year's supply of candles.

After bidding farewell to Simeon, Mary and Joseph began the journey home. On the way they discussed the prophecies of Simeon. "What will happen next, and when?" Mary anxiously asked Joseph.

"You and I must not worry about that now, dear. Let us leave each day to God. He has taken care of us so far; we must not doubt," was Joseph's kind, reassuring reply. Nevertheless, Joseph realized that Mary's heart was anxious about Jesus. She had a mother's heart.

They could see the magnificent court of Herod in the

---

[3] Luke 2:29-32

distance. They had heard people in Jerusalem talk about how gorgeous his palace was. There were two immense halls in it where hundreds of guests could be served at one sitting, eating from gold and silver vessels.

The Jews did not like Herod. He was not their lawful ruler, but was merely appointed by the Romans. Moreover, he was wicked. He had killed members of his own family, lest they take his throne away from him. Mary and Joseph had heard these stories. They were glad to hurry past Herod's palace grounds.

Sometime after this, perhaps a year or two, a group of rich camel riders made a surprise visit to Palestine. "Noblemen from the East," said one.

"Look at their chests and saddlebags. They are from the Orient lands," said another.

"Either Persia or Arabia," said a third man. "They must have been a long time coming." A great crowd gathered around them asking where they were going, and why they had come.

To all questions the strangers replied, "We are looking for the King of kings, we are looking for the great Messiah, the new Infant King of Israel. We have seen His star in the East and are come to adore Him."

"A king? Ho! Ho! Wait until Herod hears that! There'll be trouble. He will not stand for that," the people told the Magi. These holy men were disappointed that no one seemed to know about the new King. They told the people how they had seen His star in the East and that they had recognized it as the sign that a great king was born in Israel. Day and night they had traveled for many, many months.

Everyone they passed was interested in them. "Let's follow them," one suggested. Imagine the surprise of the crowd when the caravan stopped at Joseph's humble home.

The astonishment of Mary and Joseph was even greater when they saw all this excitement around their home.

The unusual visitors introduced themselves to Joseph. They were three. One was old; he was Caspar; Melchior was middle-aged, and Balthasar was young. Joseph introduced them to Mary. She picked up her sleeping Infant and showed Him to the Magi. Instantly they dropped to their knees, adored Him and kissed His feet. He woke up, stretched His little arms, and smiled at them.

Then the royal visitors sat down and talked to Joseph and Mary. They were honest men and had great love. Joseph was thrilled at their great reverence and devotion. They told Joseph how they were watchers of the skies, and were called wise men because they knew all the science then known about the skies. They practically lived out-of-doors. They knew every star by name. Every night they went up on the housetops and high places around to see the constellations rise and set.

"We have brought gifts," said Caspar, who did most of the talking. "No one goes before a king without royal gifts. I brought the gold, in honor of His kingship. Balthasar has frankincense. It is a particularly rich and fragrant resinous gum used in religious ceremonies. This we offer to honor Him as God."

"I have myrrh for the Infant King," said Melchior, "and because of its bitter taste we offer it to honor Him as man." Joseph took these gifts and set them down on the floor. He could not help admiring their great faith. It pleased him. He told the Magi the details of the miraculous birth on Christmas Eve. It was Joseph who first taught the Magi the mystery of the Incarnation. We celebrate the visit of the Wise Men on January sixth. It is called the Feast of the Epiphany.

Was it not strange that so many unexpected things happened at Christmas? There was no room for Him who made all the world. The donkey was nearest the crib, the shepherds got to Bethlehem before the Wise Men, who themselves asked the way to Bethlehem from those who never found it. Scripture calls them Wise Men; Herod called them fools; and Christ, who made the world and everything in it, chose to become a little Child and to be poor because He loves the poor.

 Discussion Questions

1. To St. Joseph it did not seem right to put his name before the name of Jesus. What do you hold to be more important than Jesus? What do you put ahead of him?
2. On page 21, we see how Joseph registered for the census: He lists his name and his father's, Mary's name and her father's, Jesus' name and His mother's. Why did he not list himself as Jesus' father in the traditional manner?
3. What might the "great sorrow" that "would one day pierce [Mary's] heart like a sword" be? (page 23)

✝ Virtues of St. Joseph

At the Temple, Mary again "was depending on Joseph" (page 22). Like Mary, we too must rely on St. Joseph. Memorize the following prayer to him and recite it daily: "St. Joseph, take care of me just as you took care of Jesus and Mary. Watch over me, protect me, guide me to your Son. Help me to pray to you when I need help. Amen."

Chapter Four
Crocodiles and Cats

AFTER a week, the Magi went home. "Surely, there can be no more extraordinary visitors," said Joseph to Mary.

"Why should we not go back to Nazareth?" Mary suggested. "I love Bethlehem, but my heart is in Nazareth. Besides, it will be easier for you to get work again among our old neighbors," she added.

"Well, that's a very good idea. I have a few odd jobs to finish, but, in a couple of days we can go back," said Joseph.

That evening, as he was about to close shop, Joseph saw a man and boy coming up over the hill. "I had better wait; they may be needing something." It was old Isaac who had come with a broken plowshare. Plows broke easily in Palestine's rocky soil. There was no steel or iron tip to guard the point of the wooden plow. "Can you do this right away?" asked Isaac, "I want to use it as soon as I can."

"Yes, I can do it. I have just the right kind of wood on hand for this," said Joseph. "Come back this time tomorrow. It will be ready." Isaac was pleased.

Joseph got down his saw again. He dug under several heavy beams of wood for the special, tough-fibered kind needed for heavy repair work of this type. "It is too dark to work much longer, but I will cut off this length, and leave everything ready for an early start tomorrow. I must not disappoint Isaac," Joseph thought.

After supper that night, Joseph asked Mary to call him earlier than usual in the morning. It would take all day to fix a plowshare. Mary promised that she would have breakfast ready early. She always helped Joseph in his plans.

Joseph slept soundly that night. He was especially tired. While he slept, an angel came to him. He shook St. Joseph and called him. He had to call twice. "Joseph, wake up!" he said. Joseph woke with a start. He was astonished to see an angel standing over him. "You have to get away from here. King Herod is searching for the Holy Child. You must fly to Egypt with the Baby and His mother," said the angel. "Hurry! Get the donkey ready." By this time, Joseph was wide awake. He repeated the angel's orders. "Rise, take the child and his mother, flee to Egypt, and stay there until I tell you."[4]

Notice that it was to Joseph the angel spoke this important message. Many thoughts must have entered his mind. "Fly," the angel had said. "Now? In the middle of the night? Can't I wait until the morning? Why didn't you come earlier? Take my wife and Child? Impossible! They need their sleep. Don't you know that it is bad to take a baby out of a warm bed into the cold damp air of night? Besides, it would worry His mother. I can't do that just now. *Fly!* Why I don't even know the way. I have never been over that road. Egypt is hundreds of miles away. I do not know anybody there. Doesn't an angel realize that I have to support the Family? How can I do so in a strange land? I do not even know the language of the place. How will I get new customers? How long will I have to stay? It makes all the difference in the world to me. Then, too, there's Isaac's

---

[4] Matthew 2:13

plowshare. I gave him my word of honor to have it done for him tomorrow evening!"

Scripture does not state that Joseph said any of these things in reply to the angel. It tells us that he "rose and took the child and his mother by night and departed for Egypt."[5] He did not wait until the next day to do what he was told to do. He rose at once and roused Mary. They dressed quickly and packed a small bundle of things. Only the donkey rebelled. He did not like getting out in the middle of the night at all. But when he found out that King Herod was searching for Jesus, he said: "Herod wants to kill Him? Oh, that's different. Why, certainly, I will go, Joseph. Swing up that bread bag on my back, and the waterskin, too. Dry bread is not so tasty, you know. Be sure the Blessed Mother is well seated. The saddle was a bit shaky at Christmas. I want her to look well, too. I am a very proud donkey. Not every donkey is chosen to carry the Holy Child Jesus and His mother. Count on me, Joseph; I will do my very best to help you. Please don't forget a little oats!"

By this time our Lady was ready. She had packed some bread, figs, olives, and, of course, a measure of feed for Donkey Oaty. St. Joseph extinguished the fire. They bolted the door and stepped out into the dark night. Long before daybreak the Holy Family was well on the road that led south to the land of pyramids and pharaohs.

The flight into Egypt must have taken at least a month. It was a slow, tedious journey of hundreds of miles. Great fear filled Joseph's heart, knowing they were in constant danger of being discovered by the searching parties Herod had sent out to capture Jesus. Every hoofbeat of a donkey behind them startled him. A face suddenly appearing from

---

[5] Matthew 2:14

behind some vineyard wall increased his fear.

Before them were hot desert miles. Our Blessed Lady shielded Jesus' eyes from the white glare of the sand. But St. Joseph had to face it most of the time. It made his eyes sore. Even Donkey Oaty was almost blinded by the hard glare. To add to the animal's troubles, he sometimes stumbled into long dips in the desert, which is never flat for long. On and on they traveled through thick, wooded hills and down into hot, windless valleys. But, no matter how hot the day, evenings brought relief. When the sun went down, night followed promptly. There is no twilight in Egypt. A bright red sky turns to a dull gray pink; a few timid stars peek out. There is a pause of ten minutes, then suddenly, night swoops down on the earth and all the stars come out to see.

Now, there would be cool rest. Joseph built a small twig fire, heated some milk, and they ate their little meal. By this time, Joseph was utterly exhausted. He spread out the rugs, and they went to sleep.

In the middle of the night Joseph got a bad fright. A loud howl woke him up. His first thought was that it might be Herod in pursuit, or, perhaps, it was a robber band that had come upon them. Often travelers were molested by thieves known as tomb robbers. They believed that all travelers through the desert were after the gold that was buried with the old pharaohs. These tombs of the pharaohs were often broken into for the wealth buried there—for the gold cups, vases, ornaments, and jewelry. Alas! It was only Donkey Oaty that had been bitten by a sand flea. He brayed so loudly that he could be heard in Jericho. Of course, he was sorry when he found that he woke up the Baby. "Well, you see, there He's crying now. That's what happens when you take a very young Baby on a long trip.

I do not approve of it at all." But he promised himself that he would be more careful.

Only one other time did Oaty get excited. That was when they came upon a pile of whitened bones, the carcass of a camel, in a very parched region. He stopped right in his tracks. He just would not go on until Joseph had scattered the ghostlike pile. Long stretches of black soil made Donkey Oaty very happy for he was a very intelligent donkey. He knew that an oasis was near, and that meant dates—fat, luscious dates—especially the rich mahogany-colored ones!

Sometimes, the Holy Family stopped at night in khans, or inns. These were nothing more than rough stone shelters used by travelers. Legend tells us that at one of these places our Blessed Mother wanted to bathe the Baby Jesus. There was another woman there, too, who had a baby the same age as Jesus. This baby was sick and diseased. "Oh, if my child were only well and lovely looking like yours," the distressed mother said to Mary. "If you will let me bathe him in the water in which your Infant is washed, I do believe he will be cured, and become strong." Our Blessed Mother felt sorry for this poor woman who was so worried about her sick child. This woman, of course, did not know who our Blessed Mother was, nor who her Child was, but she felt that they were different from and more beautiful than any other people she had ever seen.

What happened to the sick baby? He was cured, and grew strong. Alas! When he was a young man, he followed his father's trade—he became a robber! Like all robbers, he got caught. He was sentenced to death by crucifixion, which was a common penalty in those days. The date set for the crucifixion was the Friday before the Feast of the Pasch, on the hill of Calvary.

His mother went with him up to Calvary. Whom do you

suppose she met there? Mary! How sorry she was to hear that Jesus, too, was sentenced to death. She could not understand it.

Suddenly, she heard her son's voice. "Jesus, remember me when you come into your kingdom."[6]

Again, Mary's Son grants a favor. "Amen, I say to you, today you will be with me in Paradise,"[7] He said to the man on His right, around whose neck hung a board on which was written, "Dismas—robber—caught on the Jerusalem-Jericho road."

We do not know whether Joseph entered Egypt by the city of Alexandria or not. This marble city of Cleopatra had been a famous, wealthy city—an important capital like New York, Paris, or London. If it were through this port that the Holy Family entered, we may be sure that they would have hurried out of the city quickly. The idolatry of the place would have saddened Joseph. Everything was worshiped here—except God. Bulls and crocodiles were venerated. Cats, too, were kept for sacred worship, and were fed on "divine mice." There are different places mentioned as the spot where the Holy Family lived while in Egypt. Some think they lived in the ancient city of Heliopolis, about six miles from Cairo. Today, Heliopolis is a big city with a large international airport. Nothing remains of the ancient site except one obelisk. This was a part of the Temple of the Sun, where Moses may have been educated. There are two other obelisks from the same temple—one in London, the other in New York. This latter one is called Cleopatra's Needle. Who knows but what the Boy Jesus ran and played about it during the exile?

---

[6] Luke 23:42
[7] Luke 23:43

> Little Jesus close your lids
> In the shade of pyramids.
> Cuddle to Your mother's breast
> Fear is fled, now calmly rest.
>
> O'er the burning Afric sand,
> Into Egypt's bondage land
> Where our sainted fathers slaved,
> E'er the God of justice saved.
>
> Jesus, must it ever be
> Pain and poverty for Thee?
> Oh, my love would build a throne,
> Richer than the Pharaoh's own,
> I, a lowly carpenter, would build
> Of precious stones, where we Three
> Might live alone.[8]

The Holy Family began housekeeping again. They found a few Jewish families there. When Antony had given Cleopatra some very valuable balsam groves in Jericho, she rented them to Herod for about one hundred and twenty thousand dollars a year. She liked balsam so much that she had some transplanted to Egypt. In this way Jewish gardeners and their families went with her to Egypt.

One Jew helped Joseph to get a house to rent. It was a low, flat-roofed house. Another family gave Joseph some palm matting and a bench. Then Joseph cut a window that looked out north toward the Temple in Jerusalem.

One of the first things the Holy Family did was to make a thank-offering in the synagogue for their safe arrival. Then Joseph bought some tools and set up a shop at the end of a narrow street.

---

[8] From *Give This Man Place* by Father Blunt (Union City, N. J., Sign Press).

Business was very slow. Mary helped to earn a little by spinning and needlework. She also learned to make palm mats and water baskets out of the tough date-tree fibers. In Egypt, people depended a great deal on the date tree. The trunk gave wood for building and fuel, the fronds were used for fences and roofs, and there were many ways of using the date itself for food. Joseph prayed for work.

It was not all sadness and difficulty for Joseph. He had some joys in Egypt. One afternoon, as he turned up the street, he saw Mary standing in the doorway, unusually happy. Jesus was wearing His first little suit or dress. And, oh! He was walking! His first steps! It was in Egypt, too, that Jesus first started to talk. Joseph loved teaching Him the simple, holy words of the Hebrew Scriptures.

It was not long before Jesus was walking to the shop. "I must make a seat for Him on the bench," he said. Like other boys, Jesus did not stay very long on the bench. He would slip down, run around the shop, and take great delight in scuffing up the curled shavings. Once He got a nail in His little sandal. "Oh, I must watch out. These little feet are far too young for nails," said Joseph. After that, Joseph was very careful and never left nails scattered on the floor.

> Whenever the bright blue nails would drop
> Down on the floor of the carpenter shop,
> St. Joseph, prince of the carpenter men,
> Would stop to gather them up again;
> For he feared for two little sandals sweet,
> And very easy to pierce they were
> As they pattered over the lumber there
> And rode on two little sacred feet.[9]

---

[9] From the poem "Nails," in *In Towns and Little Towns,* by Fr. Leonard Feeney (New York: America Press).

Joseph often went down to the riverbank for timber. Sometimes he took Jesus with him. While Joseph cut logs, Jesus would pick blue water lilies for His mother. One day, Joseph suddenly realized that the Child had been gone too long. Quickly, he dashed around the bend of the river. There was the Child Jesus talking to a huge sixteen-foot crocodile! "Gracious!" exclaimed Joseph, "It's a wonder You didn't get bitten. This crocodile is very hungry. He has not eaten for six months. This is his eating season. Let's go home. He does not care for water lilies. He prefers fish."

How long did the Holy Family stay in Egypt? Some say it was seven or eight years; some say it was three years. We do not know. We only know that the exile ended when Herod died. "Stay there until I tell you,"[10] the angel told Joseph. As he had promised, the angel appeared to Joseph when Herod died, and said, "Rise, take the child and his mother and go to the land of Israel, for those who sought the child's life are dead."[11]

Mary and Joseph were glad to be going home again. Joseph was a patriotic man who loved the fatherland. They gave the last of their provisions to some poor who had come to beg. These poor were sorry to see the Holy Family go. Mary had been very kind to them, and Joseph had often made furniture and done repair work for them for free.

They took the route that followed along the Mediterranean seacoast, the same way they had come. Again, Jesus is in the bleak desert, a lion-colored landscape with a hard blue sky overhead.

This time Joseph had a new worry. Jesus was older now. He was too big to be carried all the time, and not strong enough to walk for very long. Of course, Donkey Oaty was

---

[10] Matthew 2:13
[11] Matthew 2:20

quite willing to carry both Jesus and Mary, but too much cannot be expected from one donkey.

It was the same long tramp back. They were heading for Bethlehem, but Joseph was worried.

Talking it over with Mary, he found she, too, was afraid of Herod's son, Archelaus, quite as much as they had been of Herod, himself. That night an angel appeared to Joseph and settled matters. He said to Joseph, "Go to Nazareth." What welcome words to their ears, "Nazareth," their first, dear, little home.

Discussion Questions

1. Why is this chapter on the Holy Family's time in Egypt entitled, "Crocodiles and Cats"? (See pages 32 and 35.)
2. Are you ever asked to do something that you don't understand or agree with? How did St. Joseph respond to the angel's orders?
3. Why do you think Joseph was not afraid when he received messages from the angel?

Virtues of St. Joseph

When the angel asks Joseph to take Jesus and Mary to Egypt in the middle of the night, he obeys immediately without making any excuses or asking any questions. Remember the prompt and uncomplaining obedience of St. Joseph the next time you are asked to do something.

Chapter Five
Home

AFTER many long days of travel, they saw the same white houses on the rising hillsides. Donkey Oaty flapped his ears to make the Boy Jesus laugh. "He, haw! This is the finest place on earth!" he thought. "I haven't seen such nice grass for years!" Mary remarked how beautiful the gold wheat fields looked against the dark purple hills. All the flowers seemed to have come out for a welcome. There was the dear little red anemone, the rose of Sharon, and the white narcissus, or lily of the field as it was sometimes called. Even the silvery olive trees nodded as they passed.

It was early evening when the Holy Family eventually reached their little home in the hills. A silver moon shed a soft light on everything. Joseph could hardly find where the door had been, so high and thick had grown the weeds. Before going inside, he knelt to thank God for a safe return. The walls within the house were very damp. Some of the plaster had dropped off. Little Jesus quickly explored the place and found a bird's nest. The birds were frightened, but with a few grains of corn He induced the mother bird to stay.

That night, when Mary covered the Child Jesus, she tucked Him in tighter than ever. Even Joseph peeked in twice; it seemed so good to know He was safe in the little white house they loved.

The next morning, when neighbors saw smoke again coming from Joseph's chimney, they hurried to welcome the family home. They had believed that Joseph and Mary were dead. They saw Jesus! Oh, how surprised and happy they were. What a beautiful Child He was! Joseph was very proud of Him, too. He could have gone around telling them about the wonderful events connected with Bethlehem, the Magi, and Egypt. But he did no such thing. He would let Mary tell whatever details she cared to relate. At this time neither of them felt that they should explain why they had stayed in Bethlehem after the enrolling, or about their journey to Egypt. To tell everything now would be to reveal the mystery of the Holy Child. It was not yet time to do so.

Joseph's sister, Mary, who was married to Cleophas, lost no time in coming to see them. She had much to tell Joseph about his father's death. She brought Joseph's portion of his father's money. At first, Joseph would not take it. His first thought was, "I am rich enough with Jesus and Mary." But, when he realized that he would need a little to buy some new tools, he consented to take the silver, but not the gold.

The next morning, Mary hung the washing on the old, familiar thorn bushes. Friends came again to the house; old acquaintances were renewed, business picked up, and things took shape again, just as they had been before.

Joseph was sitting outside, one evening, when a weary traveler plodded toward his door. "Good evening, I am glad I made your place before night," he said to Joseph. "I have been all day getting this far from Capernaum. I am on my way to Naim."

"Good," said Joseph. "You are just in time to come in with us for supper. There are few houses from here out among the hills. You will like our barley loaf, and we have the best goat's milk for miles around," urged Joseph. The man decided to stay with Joseph for the night. No one could resist such a sincere invitation.

Mary had heard the conversation. Quickly, she set out two water jugs and towels, and made a fourth place at the table. Then she went to the door to welcome the guest. Immediately, the man felt at home. "What a happy home," he remarked to Mary, "and such courtesy!"

"Joseph always thinks of others first," remarked Mary.

"Bread is always the sweeter for having been shared with others," said Joseph.

In the meantime, the young Boy Jesus was growing up. How Joseph loved Him, God's dear Boy, a bright, merry Lad with dark eyes and a shock of curly hair. "He is a playful Lad, too," said Joseph one day to a neighbor. "He can outdistance any of His playmates in ball or running. I wish you could see Him with the slingshot!"

Like other boys, Jesus ran to His foster-father with difficulties—things He could not solve Himself. Of course, He was God. But He was also a little Child like other children. "Please mend My cart," He asked Joseph one night. Joseph examined the broken wheel.

"Now, Joseph, this is the second time those wheels have broken. Don't you think you had better make Him a new pair?" suggested Mary.

"Yes, I think I will. I have a small piece of Bashan oak left over from Rebecca's chest; it is just big enough for four small wheels, and too small to use for anything else. While you're getting supper, Mary, we'll go down to the shop."

"Don't be gone too long, Joseph," said Mary, "I have honey cake tonight, and it is much nicer hot," she added.

"Ym-m-m-m, you make the best honey cake around these parts, Mary. We will be back on time," Joseph promised.

Devotion to St. Joseph

Down the street Jesus and Joseph went, hand in hand. Sometimes, little Jesus stopped to pick up a pretty stone to add to His collection. These He kept in a special box that Joseph had made for His birthday.

At the shop, Joseph lifted the young Child to a nearby bench. Jesus watched Joseph closely. He loved his foster-father. He knew that Joseph was a good man. He wanted to be just like him. "Please, may I be a carpenter when I grow up?" He asked.

"Indeed, you may," said Joseph. "You will be the best carpenter we ever had in Palestine, I am sure!"

How delighted Jesus was with four new wheels.

He spun them around and up and down the wooden spike that held them. On the way home one of them rolled into the street, right into the path of a laden camel! The frightened animal upset the panniers of fruit he carried. The driver grew very angry and hollered at St. Joseph, "You stupid man, get that boy out of the way. See my fruit spilled in the mud!"

"I am sorry, neighbor," said the gentle Joseph as he helped to pick up the fruit. They were very nice oranges, too. Secretly, he wished he could have two, one for Mary and one for Jesus. There was nothing Jewish people liked better than juicy Jaffa oranges! "I will do some repair work for you to make up this loss, or, I will barber the camel for you," Joseph offered. Barbering a camel was a long, dirty job. It was done before the great heat set in. It meant shaving, oiling, and smearing the animal with mud. The camel man ignored Joseph. Even the camel looked peeved, a bit haughty and scornful (as camels always look).

According to the Jewish law the father was the teacher of his son. He had to find time every day for that duty. Even during harvest time, when they had little time even for meals and sleep, some time had to be devoted by the Jewish father to teaching the prayers, psalms, and Scripture texts. There were long passages to be memorized, and stories of Abraham, Moses, and Sampson to be learned.

Every evening, after supper, Joseph took the parchment scrolls from the wooden box that was nailed just inside the door and went out into the courtyard to hear Jesus recite. Of course, he did not quite understand why he should be teaching Jesus, who he knew was the Son of God. However, St. Joseph did not question about it. He was the father of the household, and he would fulfill the duties of a father.

In this way Jesus learned from Joseph the lessons about God who made the world, and who wishes even the smallest boys and girls to tell the truth, to be good and gentle, and to obey their parents.

 Discussion Questions

1. How do you feel when you come home after spending a few days or a week away? How do you think Joseph and Mary felt after spending years away?
2. St. Joseph did not tell anyone about the wonderful things that had happened since he was away. How hard is it not to tell someone something that you are excited about or something you did? Why do you think Joseph didn't tell anyone the wonderful things that had happened in Bethlehem and Egypt? Why didn't he tell about what happened with the Wise Men?
3. See how welcoming Joseph was to the weary traveler (pages 38-39). How do you treat strangers? Do you greet

them politely? Do you try to take care of their needs? Discuss how you can become more welcoming.
4. "Bread is always the sweeter for having been shared with others" (page 39). What does this mean? What lesson does this saying of St. Joseph's teach us?

✠ Virtues of St. Joseph

"Joseph always thinks of others first" (page 39). Can people make that statement about you? If not, what can you do differently to change that? Name at least two ways you can imitate St. Joseph by putting other people's needs and feelings before yours.

Chapter Six
A Holiday Crowd

Mary remarked, one evening as she went to the cupboard for the oil jug, "Joseph, dear, we need more oil. It is surprising how this lamp eats up fuel."

"Last year, up at Jerusalem, I saw a new kind of torch oil on the market," said Joseph, "and it is much clearer than this thick, smelly stuff. We'll be going up next week. Jesus, too, will be going this year; He is twelve now. He can help to carry some purchases."

There was a little tug at Mary's heart. She could hardly believe her Boy had grown old enough to be bound by the law of Moses which prescribed that every Jewish man make a pilgrimage to the Temple three times a year. The first pilgrimage was the Feast of the Pasch.[12] This was in memory of the preservation of the first-born of the Jews. The feast lasted seven days. Seven weeks later came the Feast of Pentecost. This commemorated the day that the Israelites received the Law on Mount Sinai. The third pilgrimage came in autumn. It was called the Feast of Tabernacles in memory of the time when the people lived in tents. It was a thanksgiving feast for all the fruits and blessings of the year. Those who lived at great distances fulfilled the law by one visit a year—at the Feast of the Pasch or Passover.

---

[12] Jewish Feast of Passover

Year after year, Joseph had gone to the Temple to make his yearly visit. He was a real Jew. He was not satisfied with anything but the fulfillment of the Law. He would like to have gone more than once a year, but he could not take the time from work. He might have excused himself from the law. He could have said he did not need to go to God; he had God in the house with him every day. But, no, that would be giving bad example to the neighbors. He would keep the Law, cost what it might.

So, one bright spring morning, Joseph and Mary joined the caravan from Nazareth. This year Joseph had a new joy. He was taking Jesus with him. God's own Boy was now a man. Children in the East were older for their years than children in the West. Roman boys put on the toga at fourteen; a Jewish boy became a man at thirteen.

Despite the hardships of travel in those days, it was a joyous time. Old friends met, and families who had not seen each other all year were united. There was much noise and excitement in the crowds of olive growers, fishermen, merchants, men and boys, maids and their mothers. They traveled in one huge caravan for safety against fierce brigands that hid in the hills. Even today, robbers roost along the lonely road from Jericho to Jerusalem. There is a hotel there now called the "Good Samaritan Inn," recalling the parable that Christ told of the Good Samaritan.

They rode a long way to the east, pitching their tents at night by the River Jordan. In this way they avoided the country of the Samaritans, who were enemies of the Jews. At last, the dazzling roof of the Temple shone in the sun on the summit of Mount Olivet. Shouts of joy went up from the holiday crowd. Loud bursts of psalm singing filled the air.

In the city of Jerusalem, there was great commotion among the throngs of pilgrims. Roman soldiers swaggered about the streets, armored and helmeted, with shining spears. They jostled the Jews who drew back out of their way. The rich rode in cushioned litters, or in rumbling carts of brass and jingling metal. Caravans of heaped-up crates paraded around. They were loaded with spices, wood, fruits, silks from Damascus—which is sometimes called the world's oldest city—ivories, pottery, and perfumes from Persia, now called Iran.

The Feast of the Pasch lasted seven days. During this time the pilgrims attended the different services in the Temple, visited, and saw all the sights.

There was shopping to do, too. Rows of open booths with piles of yellow and red fruit, fragrant herbs and fresh greens, all thrown together, enticed purchasers. Groups of women gossiped over heaps of gold thread, clasped sandals, ornaments, bracelets, and belts. Men gathered at the stalls of bronze-faced stonecutters. Joseph, too, was fascinated to see these craftsmen cut and chisel bright stones and place them in metal settings. He was a careful worker himself, and he valued good careful workmanship. "This is exquisite work," he remarked to a bystander.

Further along were wicker crates containing apes and rare birds. Greek merchants showed the sandalwood, alabaster boxes, and settim tables. From time to time, one of them sprinkled a mixture of aloes and myrrh or oriental terebinth and spikenard into a glowing charcoal brazier. There were the noisy money-changers, too! Because so many people came great distances to the Holy City on feast days, often they waited until they got to Jerusalem to buy their doves, lambs, and other things which they were to offer in the Temple. This meant there was much buying and selling. Many of these Jews came from foreign cities, and so they had to have their coins and bills changed into the kind that was used in Jerusalem. Often there were arguments, especially if a man thought he had been shortchanged.

The smell of heavy, meaty stews reminded Joseph that it had been a long time since he had eaten. The sun was now high in the heavens. Scanning the groups of women, he singled out Mary. They were both glad to leave the bellowing street venders and the deafening noise of the densely crowded market place.

They headed for a quiet place to eat near a cool stream. Joseph spread out a napkin full of fresh bread, some herbs and wine, and a surprise package of sugar-coated almonds for God's dear Boy, as Joseph so often called Jesus! Joseph was happiest when he was doing something for Jesus and Mary.

After the days of the solemnity, the Holy Family set out for home with the Nazareth caravan. They had offered a sheaf of grain, the first produce of the new harvest. They had eaten the unleavened bread, bread without yeast, to show their hearts were pure, and to remind them of the hurried departure from Egypt that their forefathers made with Moses. For the same reason, they had eaten the roasted lamb, eaten it standing as if ready for a similar departure. Now they would return home until next year. Goodbys were said, and everyone set out for his own town caravan.

There was just as much commotion getting ready to go back as there had been in coming. The roads leading out of Jerusalem were crowded for many miles. It was noon before the pilgrims got started. They rode hard until nightfall. When the stars came out, the entire multitude got out and prepared to camp out for the night. Much confusion was caused by some setting up tents, while others prepared the evening meal. Husbands came looking for their wives, and children ran noisily around rejoicing at the prospect of camping under the stars. Joseph and Mary met. Each of them was alone! Jesus was missing! He was lost! No one had seen Him! Mary thought He was with Joseph; Joseph thought Jesus was with her! Suppertime came and went. Bedtime came, and no Jesus! They went here and there among the crowd with a lighted torch. Two hours pass, three hours go by. The people are getting cross with Joseph for disturbing them. "Don't be bothering us; we want to sleep. If your boy were anywhere in this multitude, He would have gone to you before now." Joseph looked at Mary, she, at Joseph.

"He must be still in Jerusalem," said Joseph, "let us go to Him."

The Paschal moon still shone brightly, giving light to Joseph and Mary along the road. Every time they saw a boy the size of Jesus their hearts leaped. Mary remembered the words of holy Simeon. Terror seized her, and Joseph shared it. He blamed himself for it. He had failed to guard the Holy Child as God had expressly asked him to do. "Yes, I am the head of the Holy Family; this is my responsibility. I have lost Him for whom I was appointed guardian! And this, after having been ordered by an angel to take Him to Egypt because threats had been made upon His life! Oh, I have had many sorrows and hard days, but this is the worst trial, to be without Jesus."

Again we find Joseph a man of action. "I will not rest until I find Him," he vowed.

After many uneasy hours, Mary and Joseph reached the city again. They asked the gatekeeper and the guards if they had seen Jesus. They inquired at the house where they had eaten the Paschal lamb, and at many shops. No one had seen Him. They would try the Temple. Through porches and porticoes they went. Mary hears a voice. She is startled! Joseph put a protecting arm around her. They stand and listen. There is no mistaking that voice. It is Jesus'. They walk in further. There He is, seated in the middle of the floor surrounded by the doctors of religion. He is asking questions, but no one seems to be answering. Every eye is fixed upon Jesus. No one sees them. Mary looks at Joseph with a smile when she hears Jesus answering His own questions. One by one the ancient and wise elders leave the Boy Teacher, astonished at His great wisdom.

Jesus is alone. He sees Mary and Joseph approaching. With tears in her eyes, Mary says, "Son, why have you done this to us? Your father and I have been looking for you with great anxiety."[13] Joseph had been greatly disturbed for three days, yet, he did not burst into anger at Jesus. There was no arguing; no useless talk, no blaming one another.

Jesus answered, "Why were you looking for me? Did you not know that I must be in my Father's house?"[14] They did not quite understand this. But they knew that Jesus was God, that He would not act unwisely. God did not make it quite plain to either Mary or Joseph the reason for this, but they worried no more; they had found Jesus. So, too, we may not always understand why God allows some things to happen to us, but if we have found Jesus, it will not matter. We will find Jesus with Mary and Joseph, for these three cannot be separated. We cannot think of one without the others. Say often, "Jesus, Mary, and Joseph, I give you my heart and my soul."

What a difference it made to Mary and Joseph to have Jesus with them. Joseph had found Jesus, and, although

---

[13] Luke 2:48
[14] Luke 2:49

it had been a keen suffering to be without Him, Joseph was extremely glad that others had found Him, too. Joseph, ever generous, was glad to share Jesus with others. We should remember this, and pray to St. Joseph often. Never forget he is with Jesus, and Jesus is with Joseph. On Wednesdays, say some special prayer in his honor. This is the day the Church gives him.

 Discussion Questions

1. When He was thirteen, Jesus—as a Jew—was bound by law to go to the Temple in Jerusalem to celebrate the Feast of Passover. What "rites of passage" do you—as a Catholic celebrate? At what age do you celebrate certain sacraments and celebrations of our Faith?
2. Joseph went to Jerusalem once a year in order not to "give bad example" to his neighbors. What does this mean? In what ways might you give "bad example" to others?
3. "Joseph was happiest when he was doing something for Jesus and Mary." (page 46) Can the same be said about you? What can you do to better imitate St. Joseph in this regard?
4. Joseph and Mary worried when they lost their Son, Jesus. They blamed themselves. What does Joseph mean when he says, "I have had many sorrows and hard days but this is the worst trial, to be without Jesus"? (page 47) What would it be like to be without Jesus? What actions can we take to prevent losing Him?
5. Imagine the worry of Joseph and Mary as they searched for Jesus for three days! Yet, when they found him,

Joseph "did not burst into anger at Jesus. There was no arguing; no useless talk, no blaming one another" (page 48). How can you imitate St. Joseph in controlling your anger? What does he teach us about blaming others? What does he teach about the value of careful words—and silence?

✝ Virtues of St. Joseph

St. Joseph, ever generous, wants to share Jesus with us. He is a powerful intercessor in heaven; he is there with Jesus and can help us in our needs. Write your own prayer to St. Joseph to honor him every Wednesday. Think about what you most admire about St. Joseph. Consider how he lived his life and the lessons you can learn from him. Write a few short sentences asking him to help you become more like him in at least two ways. If you wish, you can compose a poem to St. Joseph to use as a prayer.

Chapter Seven
The Good Man on the Hill

JESUS went back with His Mother and His foster father into Galilee. As He grew older, He swept the floors and helped Mary to wash the dishes. Often neighbors would remark how thoughtful He was. If Mary or Joseph dropped anything, He ran to pick it up. How happy they were with their Boy!

After the first attendance in the Temple, a Jewish boy began to learn his father's trade. So Jesus went into the carpenter shop. He stood by Joseph's side, watching carefully how things were made. He listened attentively to the directions that Joseph gave when He took the tools in His own hands. Joseph's strong and steady hand guided the less steady one of the young Boy Jesus in the use of the plane. How the angels must have looked down in wonder to see how carefully and obediently Jesus worked under Joseph! Can we fail to realize how important St. Joseph was when we see Jesus, who is God, obeying him? Indeed, Joseph is the greatest saint in heaven after our Blessed Lady.

Years passed. Jesus was now a young man. He was tall, athletic, and strong. Mary was busier now than ever. She had two leathern jerkins to mend; there were rest mats and linens for two men to make now. She had to bake more often now, too.

Joseph, however, could take things a little easier now. He had worked very hard all his life. He was getting old.

He was glad to have Jesus to help him, especially with the heaviest work.

Joseph was glad to have Jesus help him, especially with the heaviest work.

One day, as Mary put the finishing touches to the evening meal, she heard something she had not heard before. A heavy, weary step thumped alongside the house. She wondered for an instant whom it could be. Leaning out the window, she saw Joseph turning in at the door. A pang of sorrow and worry struck her heart! "Joseph must be sick," she thought, "I had not realized that Joseph was getting old so rapidly."

"This was a hard day," Joseph said. "My, but I am glad to get in." Then, looking at the table, he said, "Smells like something really good." He hung up his coat, washed, and sat down. Mary lit the lamp. Jesus came in.

"Did I keep you waiting, Mother? I went down to Reuben's with that chest Father made for Rachel!" His eager, young eyes swept the room. His favorite pudding was set out for Him. "Oh, Mother, you are such a good cook!" Joseph was very quiet. Jesus noticed it. Mary and He exchanged glances when they saw that Joseph ate very little.

"I think I shall lie down for a while," said Joseph. Jesus fixed the low couch and Mary spread a clean white coverlet on it. Jesus sat down on the low stool beside him.

After a few minutes, Mary brought a little soup on a small wooden tray, hoping to coax Joseph. But he shook his head. His appetite was gone. Days passed and Joseph did not get any better. He spent most of the time on the couch. In the evenings, when Jesus came home, He would hold the rough, brown, work-hardened palm of Joseph in His. Mary would try to tempt the sick man with choice bits of fresh fruit. Joseph would smile and thank her, but he just could not eat.

Joseph had had a hard life, with the usual joys and sorrows of most men. There had been much love and peace in it. Yet, he would have to endure sickness and death like all other people. We do not know how long Joseph was sick. Mary and Jesus did what they could to make him feel comfortable. They called the village doctor who prescribed bitter herbs steeped in water. Mary hated to make Joseph drink it, but Joseph made it easy for Mary by smiling every time she entered the sickroom with the horrid-tasting potion.

Joseph would not let Mary sit up at night with him. There was no need of it, he thought. To please Mary he let her move her cot close to his. Every time he woke, Mary was standing over him. This worried him. She had so much to do. Besides, she was in and out of his room all day with a drink, some fruit, or a cool cloth for his brow.

There was one worry Joseph did not have, and that was the care of Mary after his death. He had taught Jesus all the points of the carpenter trade. Jesus would be able to care for His mother.

Still, Joseph found it very hard to die. Other saints died gladly because they knew that they went to God, with Jesus and Mary, forever. But Joseph would have to go to limbo. He would have to endure a weary waiting for them. He had lived with them, worked for them, come and gone with them wherever they went. Now he would have to be without them.

Jesus knew Joseph's thoughts. He spoke lovingly to Joseph and told him the separation would not be for very long. Joseph fell asleep while Jesus was talking. Jesus kissed him on the forehead. Neighbors came to the door to inquire about the patient, but no one but Jesus and Mary entered the sickroom. "We will miss this good man on the hill," they said.

Later, Jesus and Mary took their evening meal together and said their night prayers together. Jesus went to His room and fell asleep quickly. Mary heard His deep breathing. She was glad, knowing that Jesus had to go to work in the morning.

"I think I will peek in again," she said to herself. As she

did so, she noticed a decided change in Joseph. She hurried out for Jesus, telling Him that Joseph was dying. Tears filled her eyes. Joseph spoke in a weak voice. He begged for blessings from Jesus and Mary. They kissed his hand; Jesus was on one side of the couch and Mary on the other. A light came into Joseph's eyes! He wanted to get up, but was too weak. Instead, he raised his hand and blessed them as was the custom of Jewish fathers. He tried to speak.

Turning to Jesus, Joseph looked long and lovingly at Him. Jesus pressed Joseph gently to His Heart. Mary clasped his other hand; he looked at her again, and then once more he gazed into the eyes of Jesus. . . . A brief moment passed . . . and the soul of Joseph had passed into limbo.

> Hope of the dying, Joseph dear,
> Forget not when I'm dying too;
> Bring Jesus and His Mother here,
> To hold me as they once held you.[15]

Jesus placed the body of Joseph in a tomb that He had prepared. After the funeral, Mary was very lonesome. She missed Joseph a great deal. She looked lovingly at his Sabbath cloak, still on the peg where he hung it last. There was his leather apron, too, with her latest patch on it, still holding firm.

She recalled many loving incidents in their lives, and dwelt affectionately upon the night that he had called her the "Gate of Heaven." She remembered having called him in return, the "Keeper of the Gate." Tenderly, she kissed his apron, folded it, and put it in the Lebanon cedar chest that he had made. Half aloud she whispered, "Dear Joseph, how well you deserved that title!"

---

[15] Father Blunt in *Give This Man Place*

*"Bring Jesus and His mother here,
to hold me as they once held you."*

We do not know how old St. Joseph was when he died, nor whether he had been sick long. His death probably took place before our Lord began His public life, as St. Joseph is not mentioned as present at the marriage of Cana. But he must have died before Christ died, because Jesus placed His mother under the care of St. John, which He would not have done if St. Joseph were living.

It is because of the happiness of St. Joseph's death, with Jesus and Mary by his side, that he is the patron of a happy death. We should pray to him for the grace of a happy death for ourselves and for all our loved ones.

Some people think that St. Joseph was not very brilliant because he was not a successful moneymaker. They consider him just a small-town carpenter of very ancient times, and not at all up-to-date. Yet, St. Joseph had a successful career. He was a wonder-worker. Mighty Herod was up in arms against him, yet Joseph won out. There was a long flight into Egypt, a wild and desolate place, yet he wrung a living out of its very deserts. He was a man of action, not a daydreamer. He was eager and alert, a man of many journeys.

They call him a silent man. Indeed, he was silent. He never boasted of his ancestry, nor did he brag about the wonderful Boy Jesus, nor did he tell others about the personal visits he received from angels, nor the important messages they gave him. He did not discuss the great hardships he was called upon to endure, nor did he argue about the way God planned things.

Often Joseph was weary, but he was no slave to poverty. He knew for whom he worked. He gloried in providing with his own hands for the comfort of Jesus and Mary.

St. Joseph was necessary to God's plans. The Holy Child needed the strong care and watchfulness of a father to preserve Him from the dangers that threatened His existence. Mary could not provide this protection because customs in the East made it hard for women to manage alone. Recall how many times in the Gospels Christ speaks of widows, and remark how kind He was to them. Moreover, as a young Nazarene growing up, Jesus needed Joseph to train Him in the duties and tasks of a man's life.

St. Joseph is the patron of homes and families. He was the head of the happiest home this world ever has seen. Ask him to bless your parents and your home. Ask him to bless America and make it a land of happy homes. Ask him to bless all the Christian families of the world, and to keep them united as one great family in God, worthy of a welcome in heaven by THE KEEPER OF THE GATE.

Discussion Questions

1. On page 51, we read, "Joseph is the greatest saint in heaven after our Blessed Lady." Why this is true? Why is it important to have a great devotion to St. Joseph? What can you do to increase your devotion to him?
2. Re-read from the bottom paragraph on page 53 through the next paragraph on page 54 about the attitude of St. Joseph while he was sick. What can you learn from his attitude?

✝ Virtues of St. Joseph

St. Joseph was the protector of the Holy Family. Ask often for his help for your family: "Gracious St. Joseph, protect me and my family from all evil as you did the Holy Family. Kindly keep us ever united in the love of Christ, ever fervent in imitation of the virtue of our Blessed Lady, your sinless spouse, and always faithful in devotion to you. Amen."

St. Joseph:
The Hidden Saint Who Served God

Winifred Sheed

St. Joseph: The Hidden Saint Who Served God

THERE are lots of ways of being a saint. Some saints have gone without food for years, and others have gone without friends. Some saints have written books, and other saints have been boiled in oil. But St. Joseph became one of the greatest saints in history simply by doing what he was told.

When God came to earth and became a man, He needed someone to look after Him at first, just as every baby does. He needed someone to take care of Him and teach Him about the world, and keep Him from harm until He was grown-up. He needed a father. And for this He chose Joseph who was an ordinary carpenter from Nazareth, which was an ordinary little town, in a place called Galilee.

God chose His parents very carefully. He chose Mary to be His mother because she was perfect in every way. And He chose Joseph to take the place of a father because Joseph had all the qualities a father needs: he was hard working, wise and strong. But, most of all, Joseph really loved God, and wanted to serve Him as well as he could. And that is what makes a saint a saint.

St. Joseph was a carpenter. In those days, they didn't have things like steel and plastic, so a man who made things out of wood was very important. He helped build houses, and he made the furniture to go in them. Nearly everything that people needed came from the carpenter, from plates to ploughs. Nowadays, many of these things are made in factories, by a lot of men working together. But in those days they were made by one carpenter, working by himself in his shop.

St. Joseph lived in Nazareth, which is called a "city" in the Bible, although now we would probably call it a small town. It had a wall around it to protect it, and big gates that were closed at night to keep out thieves and bandits. They didn't have policemen then, so they had to be extra careful after dark. In the middle of towns like Nazareth, there was usually an open square where children played. This was the market place and around it you would find the synagogue (or church) and the blacksmith's shop and the carpenter's shop and all the other important shops.

Not very much is known about the boyhood of Joseph. It is pretty certain that he became a carpenter very young. Jewish boys usually began to learn the family trade as soon as they could. Joseph's father was named Jacob, and he was a direct descendant of the famous King David, who was one of the greatest of all kings. The family of David was still held in great honor, although its members were no longer rich or powerful. People expected that one day this family would produce another great king.

So, even though St. Joseph was just an ordinary carpenter, he was also a descendant of kings. In fact, he had a better claim to be king than King Herod had. Herod did not have any royal blood at all. He wasn't even a Jew, but a member of a neighboring tribe. And Herod felt so bad about this that he set fire to all the records of the Jewish families, so that nobody would know who was who any more.

All the same, Herod was very famous, and Joseph was practically unknown. We would never have heard of Joseph at all, if God hadn't picked him out especially to be His protector. He would still have been a good man, even if we hadn't heard of him. Many saints live hidden lives, serving God in secret. St. Joseph would have been quite happy to be one of those, but God had other plans for him. As a result, St. Joseph is still known and loved all over the world, while King Herod is known only because he was ruler when Jesus was born. . . .

St. Joseph didn't look for fame. But he has become just about the most famous saint there is, with millions of children all over the world named after him every year. He didn't ask to be noticed, but he has been made the patron of the whole Catholic Church. Although he was content to stay in one tiny corner of the world, he has been made the special patron of China, Canada and Belgium. He is also the patron of workingmen, and especially of carpenters. And, of course, if you happen to be called Joseph, he's your patron, too.

But you don't have to have any special reason **to** be a friend of St. Joseph. You have only to ask him, and he'll be your companion and protector for life. Because that's the kind of saint he is.

 Discussion Questions

1. What are some qualities of a good father? Think of what the story tells us, think of your own father, think of our heavenly Father.
2. "Joseph really loved God, and wanted to serve Him as well as he could. And that is what makes a saint a saint" (page 61). What do you think makes a saint a saint?
3. From your knowledge of St. Joseph, tell what kind of a saint he was. In what way would you most like to imitate him? What favor would you most like for him to ask God for you?

✝ Virtues of St. Joseph

"St. Joseph became one of the greatest saints in history simply by doing what he was told" (page 61). Give some examples of Joseph "doing what he was told." Sometimes, we make becoming a saint very hard and think, "I could never do that!" Do you think you can become a saint by simply doing what you are told? In the Old Testament, 1 Samuel 15:22, we are told, "Obedience is better than sacrifice." In imitation of the virtues of St. Joseph, be obedient to God, to your parents, your teachers, and all other people in authority over you.

St. Joseph:
Patron of the Universal Church

Catherine Beebe

St. Joseph: Patron of the Universal Church

THE carpenter looked up from his work as the door of his shop opened. Two men came in mopping their faces from the heat of the noonday sun.

"I see you are working on the yoke for my oxen," one of the men said. "I hoped it would be finished."

"Be patient, my friend," the second man spoke before the carpenter could reply for himself. "You're always in a hurry. This man may be slow but he's a good worker and a careful one."

"You've already told me that." The first man was impatient.

"And I've also told you that there isn't a more honest man in this part of the country. But look. Your job is done."

Joseph the carpenter smiled as he handed the finished piece to the man who was waiting for it.

The customer examined the yoke thoroughly. "You are right," he said. "The yoke is strong and the wood is smooth. It will not chafe the shoulders of my beasts."

He reached into the depth of his cloak, took out his money pouch, and laid a few coins on the workbench.

"Good day, sir," he said, placing the yoke upon his shoulders. "You'll see me again when I have more work for you to do."

He hurried away, but his friend stayed. The shop was cool and pleasant. He was in no hurry to go out into the blazing sun.

"You do not charge enough for the fine work you do, Joseph," he said, seating himself on a stool near the carpenter.

"I do not need much money to live the way God would have me live," Joseph replied as he measured the wood for his next job.

"How do you know the way God wants you to live?" his friend inquired.

"That is quite simple." The carpenter talked as he went on with his work. "I keep the laws He gave to Moses and the Israelites. I serve the Almighty to the best of my ability. That is the way God wants all men to live."

"Have you no dreams, man, nor any ambitions?"

"I have both dreams and ambitions," Joseph replied. "But they are not for riches nor a high place."

"But have you no pride? You are a descendant of the great King David."

"Yes, I have pride. But it is in work well done. I have dreams, but they are of God and His angels."

The man got up from his stool and walked toward the door.

"I suppose you are going to the Temple next week," he said.

"Yes, I had planned to. I shall go with the other men of David's royal line. I shall be there on the day the high priest chooses one of us to be the husband of Anne and Joachim's daughter."

"The lovely Mary?"

"Yes. She, too, is descended from the ancient king of Israel. The law states that only his descendants may ask for Mary's hand."

"I hope you will be the chosen one, Joseph. God go with you."

The man left and the carpenter went on with his work and his thoughts.

When the time came, Joseph and the other young men

stood before the priest in the great Temple. Each one carried the staff he had used on the long walk from Nazareth to Jerusalem.

"Each of you has come to offer yourself as bridegroom for the daughter of Anne and Joachim," the priest began. "It will be difficult for me to choose one from among you. Lay your staffs upon the altar steps while I pray for God to guide me."

The young men did as they were told. The high priest stretched out his arms in prayer.

"I, too, shall pray fervently," Joseph thought. "May God grant me the honor and the joy I have come here to seek."

Suddenly, the priest dropped his arms. There was a look of wonder on his face. He walked down the altar steps and lifted one of the staffs from its place. He examined it closely, then held it up for all to see. A flower had blossomed on the top of it!

"A miracle has taken place. God has shown me by this flowering staff that he who owns it is to be the husband of Mary. Come forward then and claim it."

It was Joseph's staff. Together he and the priest walked to the home of Anne and Joachim.

After the religious ceremonies of betrothal and marriage, Mary and Joseph began the life of the Holy Family. Joseph's little house in Nazareth became their home. The Blessed Virgin took loving care of it. She prepared the meals and kept it clean while Joseph worked hard in his carpenter's shop.

Together they waited for the Baby whom the angel Gabriel had announced to Mary. The same angel had visited Joseph in his sleep to tell him of his important place in God's plan.

"The Holy Spirit has come upon Mary," the angel said.

"The Child she shall bring forth is the Son of God. You, Joseph, have been chosen by Him to protect the Mother and her Child. You shall call the little one Jesus, which means Savior, for He will save all people from their sins."

When the time came for the Son of God to be born, Mary and Joseph had to make the long journey to Bethlehem. Like thousands of other citizens, they had been ordered to go there by the emperor. It was necessary that they be counted for the census and the taxes.

It was Joseph who found a warm shelter for Mary when they learned that there was no room at the inn. It was Joseph who made a little cradle for the Christ Child out of the manger, the feed box for the cattle.

It was Joseph who watched over them when the Blessed Mother sang sweet lullabies to the sleeping Baby after He was born. It was Joseph who welcomed the shepherds and the Three Kings when they came to worship the Son of God.

Then came the time when Joseph was warned by the angel to take the holy mother and her Child into Egypt. There they would be safe from the wicked Herod who had vowed to kill the newborn King.

God the Father had placed His divine Son Jesus and His mother in Joseph's care. From the time this duty was made known to him, Joseph devoted every moment of his life to the loving protection of the Blessed Virgin and Jesus.

The same angel who warned Joseph of the danger to the Christ Child told him when that danger was over. Then Joseph took his precious charges back to Nazareth to begin again the life of the Holy Family in their little house.

It was Joseph who taught the Boy Jesus his own trade as carpenter. He taught Him all that the best father in the world could teach the Child placed in his care.

Joseph's reward for this work so perfectly done was the

highest reward anyone could receive. The foster-father of God's Son died in the arms of Jesus and Mary. No greater blessing could have come to him.

Saint Joseph is the Patron of the Universal Church. His feast day is March 19. He is the patron of carpenters. Those who ask his help in the work they are doing will surely do a more perfect job. He is the patron of all workers and is honored with a special feast day on May 1.

Saint Joseph is the one to pray to for the grace of a happy death. For every Catholic longs to return to God as St. Joseph did, in the arms of Jesus and Mary.

 Discussion Questions

1. Joseph says, ""I do not need much money to live the way God would have me live" (page 68). Discuss this idea. Give examples of how our society fights this idea. How can you fight this pressure from our American culture?
2. What are your dreams and ambitions? Compare them to the dreams and ambitions of Joseph from page 68. What can you change about your dreams and ambitions to more closely imitate those of St. Joseph's?
3. List some of the things that St. Joseph did for Mary and Jesus. What can you do to please Mary and Jesus?

✝ Virtues of St. Joseph

At the beginning of the story, St. Joseph is described as a good worker, someone who is careful in his work, someone who is honest, and someone who takes pride in a job well done. Of these four traits of St. Joseph's, choose the trait that currently least describes you. Each morning think about how you can become more like St. Joseph in that way; each night examine your day to see how well you did with this trait. Ask others to help you in your quest to become more like St. Joseph by gently reminding you when you are failing and praising you when you succeed. Pray to St. Joseph to help you to become more like him—especially in the trait you have chosen.

The Man Who Built the Secret Door

Sister Mary Charitas

The Man Who Built the Secret Door

There was high consternation in heaven. St. Peter seemed to be in some kind of excited haste as he walked rapidly in the direction of the throne room. Something had gone wrong; there was just no question about that, and he was going somewhere at no uncertain speed. He examined his keys in turn, and in turn he looked sharply into the faces of those whom he met. Once in a while, he saw some of them back off into the walls of heaven and try to escape his piercing glance as he asked of each one the same third-degree questions: "Who are you and how did you get in here? Did I see you before? Did you pass my entrance?" All of which questions were passed up without answer, except the last one. There was neither time nor opportunity even to open one's mouth before that.

Meekly each one answered: "No, St. Peter, but I came in by perfectly fair means, I assure you." Then, St. Peter would look once more most cross-questioningly, as if to ask one last accusing question, would seem to think better of it, and walk on.

Distances are very great in heaven, and even though souls there move with the rapidity of thought, because every soul moves at that same speed, a great variety of things may happen while one is walking from the door—the only door there should normally be, the Golden Gate, of course—to the throne room in the very heart and center of heaven.

St. Peter seemed to slacken his speed somewhat as he approached the throne room, as if he were thinking about the speech he was planning to make, or just how he would attempt to explain the discrepancy he had discovered some time back.

He came at last to the throne room. He went in. The words which struck his ears were these: "Enter thou into the joy of thy Lord."[16] He had admitted nobody so recently; he looked the soul in the face as she turned—another stranger had come in by some other way.

Without preliminary, he unburdened his soul: "Perhaps something is happening to my eyesight, beloved Master. I am so certain that I am never off guard, but this soul who just now went from You, she did not enter by my gate. And there must be dozens and dozens of others in heaven whom I know I have not admitted. Where in heaven do they come from? Who are they, and how do they get in?"

His Master smiled knowingly, and pointed behind the throne. St. Peter walked around that way and there—covered by a very beautiful blue drapery—was a secret door. In His usual calm and convincing voice, our dear Lord

---

[16] Matthew 25:23 (Douay-Rheims translation)

said: "St. Joseph, you see, has been at work. A carpenter still, he put in this door for his special clients. You must recognize the drapery. It is My mother's mantle, her blue one. Look sharply, and you will see where it is gathered at the top." St. Peter was satisfied. He smiled too, and tried to conceal his surprise when he met a few more souls on his way back to the main door.

Building secret doors is St. Joseph's specialty. He builds doors which lead *out* of things as well as *into* things, you know. If ever you are in any kind of trouble, no matter what the trouble is, ask St. Joseph to build you a door out of it, and he will. And it will always be a secret door, for St. Joseph spent all his life in training to master the building of secret doors; in fact, he built secretly all his lifetime, and since we continue in heaven the life we have begun here on earth, that fact explains why St. Joseph keeps right on building secret doors for folks like you and me. I am taking it for granted, of course, that you go right straight to St. Joseph when you need things fixed in your life. You should.

St. Joseph is the kind of person who followed very precisely the advice of our Savior: ". . . do not let your left hand know what your right is doing."[17]

If you read the New Testament, you will find not a single word which St. Joseph spoke. You will find the record of a few places where he was present. The single mention about him is that Joseph "was a righteous man."[18] That says just about everything, of course, but we cannot imagine *ourselves* being chosen to be the protector of the Mother of God and God's own foster-father without telling at least one of the neighbors about it. St. Joseph could do that. Nazareth was not so very large. Everybody seemed to know

---
[17] Matthew 6:3
[18] Matthew 1:19

everybody else and everybody else's business in those days even as they think they do in our own days. And yet when our Lord showed how well He knew and could interpret the Scriptures, His contemporaries were aghast and asked in utter surprise: "Where did this man get such wisdom and mighty deeds? Is he not the carpenter's son?"[19]

You see, St. Joseph had never told anybody; and yet he knew—all the time.

St. Joseph had built perhaps the very finest and most satisfying secret door for himself. That may seem strange in a man who was as unselfish as St. Joseph. But other people seem not to want this particular kind of secret door as badly as St. Joseph wanted it for himself. And yet, it is the very next bit of carpentry we must ask St. Joseph to put in for us, too. Our problem is now to work up the desire for it.

The secret door which St. Joseph had built for himself is a door into the very heart of his own heart. It is a door into the secret citadel of which Francis Thompson says, "Its keys are at the cincture hung, of God; by Him alone its floors are trod."[20] The very few people in the world who have that particular kind of secret door are able to go in and close the door behind them and so shut out the whole world, and live thereafter those exquisite moments with God alone. God dwells there all the time, but most of the time—practically all the time with most of us—He lives there alone; we never come in; we cannot because we do not have the secret door. St. Joseph will build one for us, if we want one badly enough. If you are thinking of asking St. Joseph right now, today, ask him for the grace of leading the interior life. It is not that St. Joseph would not un-

---

[19] Matthew 13:54-55
[20] From "A Fallen Yew" written in 1892

derstand if you spoke of a secret door, but *you* will understand better what he is doing when he begins work on it, if you have learned the proper terms in which to state your order.

This most important secret door is like the one behind the throne and under our Lady's mantle in heaven. They both lead *in*. St. Joseph builds every type of door leading out, too. And they are secret doors for the reason that he works so very quietly and so very gently that the door is there before you know it, but, unfortunately, without our remembering who put it there. Even when the secret door is there, we are too absorbed in the very things we want to escape from to notice that the door is there at all, and so we keep milling around and around in the disagreeable environment of trouble without common sense enough to put our hand on the knob and get out.

St. Teresa of Avila was a great one for getting St. Joseph to build these leading-out doors for her. She is one of the few people also who had him build her one of the grace-of-the-interior-life doors; and she practically never came out; she was united with God just about every moment of her life, once she had the door put in. But, about these other doors, she said one time that she does not remember having asked St. Joseph for anything, even for the least significant thing apparently, without getting it at once. You see what he did for her? He put in these doors that let her right straight out of trouble of any sort.

Part of the explanation may be, too, that St. Joseph, like any other saint including our dear Blessed Mother, always gets all his materials from God, for the saints have nothing of their own any more than we have, whether we are saints or not. Now, because St. Teresa had engaged St. Joseph to build this leading-in door to union with God, St.

Joseph was right on the job at once for any less important leading-out door she happened to want. St. Joseph knew he could depend on St. Teresa in the matter of what kind of door she would want, and that she would want always to get out of anything that had the least mark of not God about it. We are too often not so reliable, nor so sensible—sensible, meaning in this case, having common sense.

To give you some idea of the kind of situation from which St. Joseph can help you to escape, there is the matter of the young girl, for instance, who wants to be sure to meet the right man who is to become her husband. St. Joseph is a specialist in such things, having been the perfect husband to the Queen of Heaven, and the foster-father of her Child. And that is a glory and an achievement of which all carpenters, and in fact all workingmen, can always be very proud. Any girl who asks St. Joseph earnestly and with confidence to see to it that she meets the man whom God has intended for her—if she makes reasonable effort in the meantime to make herself deserving of the kind of man dear St. Joseph would select—will not be disappointed. She can depend without the least doubt on St. Joseph. Of course, it will all be done quietly; she must remember, St. Joseph is the builder of secret doors; but he builds surely and he builds lastingly.

People who want a job which is suited to their special aptitudes; folks who want to pass an examination (supposing they have studied reasonably); those who have to travel by air and want to have a happy landing; families who want to buy a house (one that is near enough to the church and school so that the children can get there each morning); people who want to sell the house they have; boys who would like to win a football or basketball game (the Child Jesus was interested in games, too, even if He never played football perhaps); girls who want to win in the singing contest; little children who want help in the building of their little Tabernacle for Jesus' first visit in Holy Communion; sinners who have gone far off the right path and want some help to find their way back to God; holy people who want to live closer and closer to God (they need a leading-in door right away)—all of these people are St. Joseph's very special interest. He has just the technique, and he knows exactly the needs of these people. If you want a job or a raise; if you want better health or more patience; if you want your garden to do well; if you need rain for the crops, or sunshine for your invalid grandmother, St. Joseph is the man who can get them for you.

St. Joseph has been allowed entry into the very treasury of heaven. He is allowed to have very much his own way with God now because of the fact that while he was here on earth he never had any will but God's. He was a very willing instrument in the hand of God.

It must have been difficult to understand why he should flee in the middle of the night with Mary and the very small Child to a country where people did not even know the true God and, of all things, to escape from Herod, a gouty old king, who had not the energy to come himself to see the newborn King Jesus when the Wise Men from the East found out for him where the little King was at the time. But there *was* no difficulty for St. Joseph to understand all this; he never even made an effort to understand it. He looked for no reasons. He had the good sense—and used it—to know that surely God always knows what He wants, and that God always wants what is best for us. If the best for everybody concerned at the moment was to flee into Egypt—however did one get there!—why, to Egypt he would go as promptly as ever he could. And that was all there was to that. God knew whether St. Joseph knew the way or not; He would guide him. Besides, he had God Himself right with him, as who of us has not? But there was nothing wrong with St. Joseph's faith; there is with ours. We don't have that very important leading-in door which St. Joseph had built for himself and which he would so gladly build for us, if we asked him.

We may be tempted to envy St. Joseph, perhaps, because he could have the Child Jesus sitting on the floor or even on his big worktable—far enough away from the big saw and things—playing around with the wood curls that came from his plane, asking him all sorts of questions about what is this for and why does he saw the boards in two, and all that. God-becoming-man is still going on in each one of us. We have no faith; that's what. We know these things; we say we believe them, but do not act like it. We live as if St. Joseph was the only lucky person way back in the year A.D. 7 or 9 and way off in Nazareth, when all the while the very same thing is going on here in our house in Chicago and Milwaukee and Crown Point and Reedsville and Richland Center.

Perhaps, because you always think of St. Joseph as very meek, very quiet and reserved, you will be surprised to learn that his most pronounced characteristic is *independence;* but that is exactly what makes him so outstanding even among the saints. St. Joseph was concerned about one single thing, and that was doing God's will as perfectly as possible. Nothing else ever bothered him, and he never bothered about anything else. What the neighbors thought of him, what the neighbors were doing with and in their own lives never kept him awake at night. If St. Joseph were living in our community today, he would not be influenced by the fact that his neighbors rode around in a fancy car or an oxcart or a limousine. He might offer his services if the contraption they had should break down and he could fix it for them, but otherwise, it would not make him buy either an oxcart or a limousine.

That is why he was so happy all his life. He did his duty as he saw it in the best way he knew and then he let the rest of the world go by. The only thing that counts anyway is that you save your soul and get to heaven, and St. Joseph set himself to that task with a right good will. He attained that goal, and now he helps out all sorts of folks who know much more than he about which stock yields the greatest dividends and which are apt to go down suddenly and which to go up if one waits a few days, but who are not too sure about the way around to the secret door which St. Joseph has built in the wall of heaven for those who have been thoughtful enough to ask him about it on time.

And that brings us to the third of the wonderful things which St. Joseph can do for us if we ask him. The first of the three is the building of the secret leading-in door that opens into our own heart of hearts; we call it the grace of the interior life—the life of union with God. The second is his wonderful independence, which he will teach us if we are interested; it is the personal love of Jesus and Mary. It makes us independent of everything except what helps to intensify that love—makes us independent of everything but God and the will of God. The third is the grace of a happy death, for which all our life must be a preparation, in fact *is* a preparation whether we know it or not, whether we want it to be or not.

That is where the secret door behind the throne comes in—the one covered with the blue drapery—the one St. Peter was so alarmed about until he understood. And if you engage St. Joseph during your life to build these other doors for you, there will be no trouble at all about finding the secret door in the wall of heaven. You see, St. Joseph is so careful about not imposing himself upon others that he never comes around with his plane and saw and says, "How would you like me to build you a door into the chamber of your heart or out of your troubles?" You must *want* such doors yourself badly enough to go and ask him. And really, all you need when you are dealing with God and holiness is to *want* things—really want them, of course—and they are yours. But that is our great trouble: we say we want things, we think we would love to lead an interior life, we want so much to be closely united with God and our Lady every minute in our lives, we would certainly like to die a very holy death, but we don't stir a hand or foot to achieve those things—all of which indicates that we do not want them with all that is in us. St. Joseph is a good person to help us want the things we should want. But we must *ask* him. By all means, let us ask him!

Discussion Questions
1. Describe the types of doors St. Joseph can build. What type of door would you like him to build for you?
2. Describe the three things St. Joseph can do for us. What would you like to ask St. Joseph to do for you?

✝ Virtues of St. Joseph
"St. Joseph was concerned about one single thing, and that was doing God's will as perfectly as possible" (page 82). Ask St. Joseph daily to help you imitate him in this one purpose in life—to please God above all others, including yourself.

St. Joseph:
Powerful Intercessor

Mary E. Mannix

St. Joseph: Powerful Intercessor

We know very little of the life of St. Joseph. It was a hidden life, and hidden lives are often holy. At the same time, we know that he was a "just man," which means that he was as perfect as anyone can be in this world.

Like the Blessed Virgin, St. Joseph belonged to the royal family of David, from which the prophet had predicted that the Messiah would be born. Although of kingly descent, St. Joseph was a tradesman, a carpenter, earning his bread by the sweat of his brow. Whether rich or poor, it was the custom among the Jews for every man to learn a trade, so that if poverty should come, they would be able to meet it. St. Joseph was poor, for our Lord wished to set an example of poverty, and so chose a man for his foster-father whose hands were hard from toil.

It is at Nazareth that we first meet St. Joseph in the Gospel. It was, and still is, an obscure town of Galilee. The name signifies "flower" or "branch." Within its walls were to bloom the fairest and sweetest flowers the world ever knew, Jesus and Mary. Coming from Jerusalem, the little town may be seen from the hills of Samaria. Its gray houses, with their flat roofs, are the same now as they were then. Here Mary and Joseph dwelt in peace and love.

. . . [After Jesus was born in Bethlehem, and after their exile in Egypt], the Holy Family returned to Nazareth. The house in which they lived was similar to those in which dwell the people of the place today. It was a square building, of brick or stone, the roof flat, with an outside railing reached by a ladder, which could be moved at will. Close to it was the carpenter shop. This carpenter shop was the first—perhaps the only—school of Jesus, where, as he planed and sawed, Joseph spoke to him of God, and taught him the Scriptures, at the same time teaching him to make plows, harrows, chairs, tables, and stools.

When Jesus was twelve he was lost for three days, and we can imagine the trouble that filled St. Joseph's soul when he could not be found. After this time we hear no more of the guardian and protector of our Lord, but it is believed that he died before Jesus began his public life.

There are many lessons to be learned from the life of St. Joseph. He was poor, and God loves the poor. He was humble, and to be humble is to possess the greatest of virtues. He had much to suffer both in body and mind during the time he lived on earth. It was his duty to take care of the two most precious jewels that had ever shone amid the darkness of the world; these jewels were Jesus and Mary. His days were a mixture of fear and joy. Fear lest something should befall his treasures—joy that he had been chosen to shelter them under his roof.

"Labor and Prayer" was the motto of his life. He joined one with the other; together they made perfection. We can always make our work a prayer. To offer every act of the day to God when we rise is to begin it well; it is to make a prayer of all we do until we lie down at night again.

St. Joseph was a silent man. We have no sayings of his on record in the Gospel. He was not a curious man. He asked no questions of the angel at any time, but did the bidding of God's messenger at once and entirely.

He is the Patron of a Happy Death, because, in the first place, he lived such a life that he could not help but die well, and, secondly, he died in the arms of Jesus and Mary, where we would all wish to breathe our last sigh. Volumes could not contain the wonderful favors which are obtained through St. Joseph. Two of these which we are about to relate are neither traditions nor legends; they have occurred during the past twenty years.[21] St. Joseph is always ready to befriend his clients,[22] and God is always ready to hear him. He cannot refuse anything to the father and guardian who now sits at His right hand in heaven.

A young man named Joseph had led a good life until the age of twenty. From his childhood he had been devout to his patron. When he left school, he fell into the company of persons who led evil lives, and little by little he began to do as they did. Among other things, he learned to drink, and soon became so fond of liquor that he seldom passed a day without being intoxicated. At last, all his friends knew him for what he was, a common drunkard.

He went to the sacraments no more—to church never. Thus several years passed, and one day while he stood in front of the cathedral watching a man haul a flag to the top of the spire, a sudden impulse led him to enter. He fell on his knees, the tears came to his eyes, and he began to sob and weep. He rose at length and went home, throwing himself on his bed, as he had felt ill all day. The next morning he could not get up; he refused, however, to take a drop of the wine which his sister offered him to steady his nerves. From that time he would not taste it. He never left his room again; he had been seized with quick consumption, caused by his bad habits. He lived three months longer. Between midnight and morning each day, he would never take anything to quench his thirst. He would say, "I have sinned through thirst, and thus I shall repent and

---

[21] Note that this was written in 1905.
[22] A client is someone who depends on the protection of another.

Devotion to St. Joseph

suffer." On the morning of the Feast of St. Joseph he said, "I think St. Joseph will come for me some time today." He died at midnight. Later it was learned that he had told his confessor he had never failed through the evil years to say, morning and evening, "St. Joseph, help me." His holy patron had not deserted him.

A man, also named Joseph, had once been rich, but had become very poor. He was not pious, but once in a while said a short prayer to his patron. At last, he was reduced to his last dollar and made up his mind to kill himself. In order to do this, he bought laudanum[23] and went to a park near the city, where he drank the contents and lay down to die, saying, "St. Joseph, ask God to forgive me." But the dose was not enough to kill him. Instead, he fell into a profound sleep and saw what he always said was a vision, though others might call it nothing but a dream. In any case, it happened.

In this dream or vision, he saw an old man coming towards him, reaching out his hand. The dreamer took it, and the old man, whom he knew to be St. Joseph, said, "Come with me." He followed, and the stranger led him into a foreign land, which looked like pictures he had seen of Jerusalem. Then he showed him all that had happened to our Lord on Good Friday, from the house of Pilate to His death on the Cross. After this, St. Joseph turned to him and said, "Jesus Christ died to save the soul you wish to damn this day," and disappeared.

The man awoke, once more took up his burden, and thanked God and his holy patron, promising to live a good life for the future. He kept his word and soon found a good situation.

Two little children, who had been taught by their good

---

[23] An alcoholic solution containing opium

mother to love St. Joseph, and who lived on the borders of a forest, where their father worked as a woodcutter, once begged to be allowed to take his dinner to him, as their baby brother was ill and the mother did not like to leave him. There were several paths leading through the forest. "My dears," said the good woman, "take the basket between you, as it is heavy, and go straight on until you come to the big oak that was struck by lightning; from that place you can easily hear the stroke of your father's ax. Follow the sound, and you will soon find him. May Jesus, Mary, and Joseph protect you." Full of joy at being permitted to go on this errand, the children started. For some distance, all went well. They kept to the path, laughing and singing. When they came to the old oak tree, they put the basket on the ground, for they had begun to feel tired. All was still. It was the noon hour, and even the birds seemed to be resting from their songs.

They turned to the right, then to the left, but heard no sound of ax or crash of falling tree. They were afraid to go out of sight of the oak lest they should lose their way.

"We cannot stay here," said the boy, at length. "Papa will be hungry, and his dinner will be cold."

"But what shall we do?" answered the girl; "we cannot hear him; he must have gone away."

All at once they heard a faint sound in the distance, and, thinking it was the noise of felling a tree, they took up their basket once more and went in the direction of the sound.

But after they had gone farther and farther into the forest, they heard it no more, and by this time there were so many little paths made by the woodcutters in their labors that they could not find their way out again. They sat down on the thick carpet of fallen leaves and looked at each other in dismay.

After a while the girl began to cry and said she was hungry. They opened the basket and ate part of what had been meant for their father's dinner. When they had finished, the sun was quite low in the sky.

"Let us pray to St. Joseph," said the boy, falling on his knees. His sister did the same, and both felt comforted. Hardly had they seated themselves on the leaves once more, when, without sound of footfall or rustle of branches, an old man appeared. It seemed as though he must have risen out of the ground.

He wore a brown cloak, but no head-covering of any kind. In one hand, he carried a staff. His hair and beard were white, his eyes dark and kindly; he smiled upon them, motioning them to rise. "It is St. Joseph!" they both exclaimed.

But the stranger did not speak. Still smiling, he made a sign that they should accompany him. They did so, and in a very short time they had wound in and out through the labyrinth of trees once more, and were at the edge of the forest, in sight of their own home, just in time to meet their father and some neighbors setting out in search of them. But when they turned to thank the old man who had led them out of the wood, he was gone. As no one knew of any such person in those parts, the villagers all agreed with the children that it must have been St. Joseph.

"I was once leaving a tenement house to which I had been summoned in an unfamiliar part of the city," said a missionary, "when I heard a voice feebly calling from a room I was passing on my way down the rickety stairs. I am a Frenchman, as you know, though for many years a resident of America. There were not many of my countrymen in L—, and I was a little surprised to hear someone ask in my own tongue, 'Who is that? Who goes there?'

"'I am a priest,' I replied. 'May the peace of God descend upon this house, and all who dwell therein.'

"'A priest!' cried the voice through the half-open door. 'Come in, Father. Come in quickly.'

"I entered. On the bed lay an old man, evidently dying. 'Father,' he said, 'I cannot speak a single word of English. The people of the house cannot understand me, nor I them. I have thought myself to be dying; now I know it, because you are here. I have always been sure that St. Joseph would not let me die without the priest.'

"I heard his confession. He had been a soldier in the French army, and had led the usual life of soldiers. After he had finished, I said, 'You have been accustomed to pray, no doubt, in some fashion during your career, to have merited this favor before death.'

"'No, Father, I have not prayed,' he said, 'but I have asked St. Joseph to pray for me. I have worn a medal in his honor all my life, and have also belonged to a Confraternity for a Good Death.'

"'You have reason to thank God,' I said.

"'If it had not been for St. Joseph,' he replied, 'I would have been left to die as I have lived, like an animal. But I have always been confident that he would be near me at the last.'

"'What is your name?' I inquired.

"'Joseph Dupre,' he replied.

"'Ah, then,' said I, 'you certainly have a double claim on the good saint. He could never have deserted you. Besides, he is the Patron of a Happy Death.'

"'Ah! Well do I know that,' he answered. 'And well do I remember how my poor old mother used to say, "Joseph, you are a very bad boy, but your blessed patron is going to stand by you at the end."

"He died the next day."

Joseph in the Old Testament was a type of Joseph in the New. *"Ite ad Joseph,"* ("Go to Joseph,") said Pharaoh to his people in the Old Testament, when they came to him during the seven years of famine for corn. Joseph was his prime minister, who had provided for their needs during seven years of plenty, and he was now ready to help them when they clamored for food. *"Ite ad Joseph,"* says our Lord, for St. Joseph is his prime minister in heaven. Nothing that he asks will be denied, for God is a just and generous and grateful God. To the father who held Him in his arms during the Holy Infancy, who led His first steps during childhood, who was at once His guardian, protecttor, and adorer, He can refuse nothing. Let us be faithful to St. Joseph, and he will never abandon us.

Discussion Questions

1. Describe the lessons the life of St. Joseph can teach us.
2. How can our work become a prayer? How can prayer help us in our work?
3. What does it mean to be faithful to St. Joseph?

✝ Virtues of St. Joseph

Holy Scripture describes St. Joseph simply as a "just" or "righteous" man. Think what a great number of virtues are tied into this description—kind, forgiving, honest, loving, fair, etc. Pick a one-word description of St. Joseph as your nightly examination of conscience.

Poems about St. Joseph

Rev. Edward F. Garesché
Sister M. Imelda
Rev. Gerald M. C. Fitzgerald
and Rev. Frederick Faber

Poems about St. Joseph

Joseph's Thoughts

Saint Joseph is known as a silent saint. He was a good listener. We are glad of this. We can feel more confident of being heard by him whenever we pray to him.

>Jesus' words and Mary's
>Oft the Gospels tell.
>Glad we read them over,
>Pondering them well.
>Sweetnesses of heaven
>In the pages dwell.
>
>Then we gently wonder:
>"All the pages through
>Never word from Joseph?"
>Hark, the answer due:
>Jesus' thoughts, and Mary's,
>They were Joseph's, too.

– Rev. Edward F. Garesche, S.J.

In a Carpenter Shop

>A hammer went, "Bang!"
>A nail answered, "Clang!"
>and a tiny Boy sang,
>Long ago, long ago,
>In a carpenter shop.
>
>His Mother came by.
>Great joy lit her eye.
>Oh, I know! I know why.
>Long ago, long ago,
>In a carpenter shop.
>
>For Saint Joseph was there;
>And the Child in his care,

Devotion to St. Joseph

> the Lord Jesus, all fair,
> Long ago, long ago,
> In a carpenter shop.
>
> Have mercy on me,
> Blessed Mother of God.

– Sister M. Imelda, S.L.

Saint Joseph's Song

(St. Joseph had to work hard to support the Holy Family. They were poor, but very happy, as you will see in this poem.)

> Steadily I work, softly do I sing,
> For I serve a queen most fair and a little King:
> Angels' lips have told me whence my Treasures came,
> Mary is His mother, Jesus is His name.
>
> Angels oft have whispered how they envy me,
> Why the Lord has chosen thus a mystery:
> What have I to offer Him save my poverty?
>
> When the sun is setting and my work is done,
> Homeward do I hasten, and God's little Son
> Comes to rest His golden head 'gainst my tired one.
>
> Mary lifts her eyes to call me to a poor man's meal—
> Blest the bread by her hands kneaded—ever do I feel
> Deeper wonder, deeper reverence o'er my spirit steal.
>
> So my work is sweet, and I softly sing,
> For I serve a queen most fair and a little King:
> Angels' lips have told me whence my Treasures came,
> Mary is His mother; Jesus is His name.

– Rev. Gerald M. C. Fitzgerald, C.S.C.

Poems about St. Joseph

In the Carpenter Shop

Good morning, dear Holy Saint Joseph,
At work in your carpenter shop.
If I come in for a visit
Will you have time to stop?
Won't you tell me about Holy Mary
And Jesus, her own little Boy?
My, but your heart must be happy,
Just breaking with holy joy!
It must be great to see them,
Mother Mary so lovely and sweet . . .
And Jesus, Who runs to meet you
With dear little sandaled feet.
St. Joseph, I just want to ask you,
Please help me to be always good,
For I want to be with you in heaven.
Oh, how I wish that I could!

– Sister Mary Magdela, S.N.D., M.A.

Great Saint Joseph, Son of David

Great Saint Joseph! Son of David,
Foster father of our Lord,
Spouse of Mary ever Virgin,
Keeping o'er them watch and ward!
In the stable you did guard them
With a father's loving care;
You by God's command did save them
From the cruel Herod's snare.

Three long days in grief and anguish
With His Mother sweet and mild,
Mary Virgin, did you wander

Devotion to St. Joseph

Seeking the beloved Child.
In the temple you did find Him:
Oh! What joy then filled your heart!
In your sorrows, in your gladness
Grant us, Joseph, to have a part.

Clasped in Jesus' arms and Mary's,
When death gently came at last,
You pure spirit sweetly sighing
From its earthly dwelling passed.
Dear Saint Joseph! By that passing
May our death be like to thine;
And with Jesus, Mary, Joseph,
May our souls forever shine.

— St. Gregory Hymnal #93

The Patronage of St. Joseph

O blessed Saint Joseph, how great was your worth,
The one chosen shadow of God upon earth,
The father of Jesus! Ah then, will you be,
Sweet spouse of our Lady, a father to me?

For you to the pilgrim are father and guide,
And Jesus and Mary felt safe by your side;
Ah, blessed Saint Joseph, how safe I should be,
Sweet spouse of our Lady, if you were with me!

When the treasures of God where unsheltered on earth,
Safe keeping was found them both in your worth;
O father of Jesus, be father to me,
Sweet spouse of our Lady, and I will love thee.

— Rev. Frederick Faber

Poems about St. Joseph

Discussion Questions
1. Why do you think that the thoughts of Jesus and Mary would be the thoughts of Joseph too?
2. What made Mary happy when she visited the carpenter shop?
3. Why was Joseph so happy with his earthly life?
4. What can St. Joseph teach us about Jesus and Mary?
5. Why do you think St. Joseph is the Patron of a Happy Death?
6. Why should we love St. Joseph in a special way?

✝ Virtues of St. Joseph
St. Joseph teaches us how sweet life can be when we live in union with Jesus and Mary. All of these poems—indeed, all of the stories in this book—show us how cheerful and joyful St. Joseph was, never complaining, always full of contentment and peace. Think how you can imitate this joyful contentment in your life. Are you usually happy? Can others feel the joy you have in your daily activities? Remember that if you are in the state of grace, you too are living each day with Jesus and Mary. Each day you share the life of grace with them. Try to imitate St. Joseph by radiating a holy joy in all you do.

Prayers to St. Joseph

I Visit Saint Joseph

Dear St. Joseph, when you lived on earth, people did not know who you were. People thought you were just a carpenter. They did not know that you were the head of the Holy Family. They did not know that you were working for Jesus, the Son of God, and God's Holy Mother. Help me, St. Joseph, to work as you did. Help me to work for Jesus, to work for Mary, to love them both. Amen.

Prayer for My Family

Good St. Joseph, you are the foster-father of Jesus. You worked for Him and took care of Him. Jesus is God, but He was obedient to you. Mary is the dear Mother of Jesus. How you and Jesus love her! You were all very kind to one another in your little house in Nazareth. We call your family the Holy Family, because you were all so good. Your home was a very happy home. Please, dear St. Joseph, help me to be obedient and kind. Help my mother and father too, so that my home will be happy; and my family, a holy family, like yours. Amen.

Prayer for a Happy Death

Dear and holy St. Joseph! You loved Jesus and Mary very much. But you could not stay with them always. One day you had to die. You were not afraid, because Jesus was there and Mary was with you too. You had a very happy death. Someday I must die too. I will not be afraid, if Jesus is with me in Holy Communion; and if Mother Mary prays for my soul. Holy St. Joseph, when you see that I am going to die, will you please ask Jesus and Mary to be with me, and will you come too? Amen.

Act of Consecration to St. Joseph

O dearest St. Joseph, I consecrate myself to your honor and give myself to you that you may always be my father, my protector, and my guide in the way of salvation. Obtain for me a great purity of heart, and a fervent love of the interior life. After your example, may I do all my actions for the greater glory of God, in union with the Sacred Heart of Jesus and the Immaculate Heart of Mary. And you, O blessed St. Joseph, pray for me that I may share in the peace and joy of your holy death. Amen.

Prayer for Wednesday
(Wednesdays are dedicated to St. Joseph.)

St. Joseph, most pure spouse of the Blessed Virgin Mary, pray for us daily to the Son of God that, armed with the weapons of His grace we may fight as we ought in this life and be crowned by Him in death. Amen.

To St. Joseph, Patron of Silence

Well may we, St. Joseph, look on you as Patron of Silence, and as teacher of the value of actions, not words. Although your good and virtuous *actions* as guardian of the Holy Child are recorded in the pages of Scripture, no *word* of yours finds place there. Were you in the mind of St. John, the beloved disciple, when he wrote, "Little children, let us not love in word, but in deed and in truth"? It is possible that you were. Your service of the Holy Child was certainly at least the type of that of which the apostle wrote.

Obtain for me, dear St. Joseph, the grace to show my love for Jesus as you showed yours—not by what I say, but by what I do.

If you ask this for me, the Holy Child cannot refuse to give it. Amen.

(Note the words of the Blessed Virgin Mary to St. Bridget of Sweden in the fourteenth century regarding St. Joseph: "St. Joseph was so reserved and careful in his speech that not one word ever issued from his mouth that was not good and holy, nor did he ever indulge in unnecessary or less than charitable conversation. . . . He rarely spoke with men, but continually with God, whose Will he desired to perform.")

Nine First Wednesdays of St. Joseph

You may make the devotion of the Nine First Wednesdays to St. Joseph in a manner similar to the Nine First Fridays to the Sacred Heart of Jesus by offering your first Wednesday Mass and Communion to St. Joseph for the intention of honoring St. Joseph and requesting a happy death for yourself, your loved ones, and those dying souls who have no one to pray for them.

Prayer to St. Joseph, the Working Man
(This prayer may also be recited on May 1, the Feast of St. Joseph the Worker.)

Dear St. Joseph, when you lived here on earth, you worked hard. You made many things in your carpenter shop. Sometimes you were very tired. But you liked to work, because you loved Jesus and Mary. Dear St. Joseph, sometimes I must work hard too. I do not always like to work. It is more fun to play. But I will try to think of you, good St. Joseph, when I have work to do. Then I will do it cheerfully. I will do my work as you did, because I love Jesus and Mary too. Amen.

A Little Litany of Saint Joseph
(For Private Use)

Saint Joseph, pray for us.
Foster-father of the Son of God, pray for us.
Head of the Holy Family, pray for us.
Joseph, most just, pray for us.
Joseph, most pure, pray for us.
Joseph, most obedient, pray for us.
Joseph, hope of the sick, pray for us.
Joseph, patron of the dying, pray for us.
Joseph, protector of Holy Church, pray for us.

Other Prayers to St. Joseph

There are numerous other prayers, litanies, novenas, chaplets, and devotions to St. Joseph. Research these on the internet or look through any prayer books that you may have.

Acknowledgements

Materials from this book were previously published as noted below. Some minor editorial revisions have been made.

Keeper of the Gate by Sister Margaret Patrice was previously published by The Bruce Publishing Company, 1941, 1945. Illustrations are by the author.
    Nihil Obstat: Edward G. Murray, DD Censor librorum
    Imprimatur: William Cardinal O'Connell, Archbishop of Boston

"St. Joseph, The Hidden Saint Who Served God" is excerpted and abridged from *Joseph* by Wilfrid Sheed from the Patron Saint Series of books for children, Sheed & Ward, Inc., 1958.

"Saint Joseph" by Catherine Beebe was previously published in *Saints for Boys and Girls*, The Bruce Publishing Company, 1959, pages 98-103.
    Nihil Obstat: John F. Murphy, Censor liborum
    Imprimatur: William E. Cousins, Archbishop of Milwaukee

The story, "The Man Who Built the Secret Door," by Sister Mary Charitas was previously published in *The Man Who Built the Secret Door*, The Bruce Publishing Company, 1945, pages 1-9. Illustrations are by the author.
    Nihil Obstat: H. B. Ries, Censor librorum
    Imprimatur: Moses E. Kiley, Archbishop of Milwaukee

"St. Joseph" by Mary E. Mannix was previously published in *Illustrated Lives of Patron Saints for Boys*, Benziger Brothers, 1905, pages 1-23.
    Nihil Obstat: Remigius LaFort, STL Censor librorum
    Imprimatur: John M. Farley, Archbishop of New York

Devotion to St. Joseph

"Joseph's Thoughts" by Rev. Edward E. Garesché and "Saint Joseph's Song" by Rev. Gerald M. C. Fitzgerald were previously published in *A Lovely Gate Set Wide* by Sister Margaret Patrice, The Bruce Publishing Company, 1946, pages 97 and 98.
    Nihil Obstat: Edward G. Murray, DD Censor librorum
    Imprimatur: Richard J. Cushing, Archbishop of Boston

"In a Carpenter Shop" and "I Visit St. Joseph" are from Sister M. Imelda's little Communion prayer book, *Jesus Bless Me* published by Benziger Brothers, 1955, pages 149 and 151. Illustrations are by the author.
    Nihil Obstat: John M. Fearns Censor librorum
    Imprimatur: Francis Cardinal Spellman, Archbishop of New York

"In the Carpenter Shop," "Prayer for My Family," "Prayer for a Happy Death" "Prayer to St. Joseph, the Working Man, and "A Little Litany to St. Joseph" are excerpted from *Welcome Jesus, A Prayer Book for First Communicants* by Rev. George M. Dennerle and Sr. Mary Magdela, The Bruce Publishing Company, 1955, pages 123-127.
    Nihil Obstat: H. B. Ries, Censor librorum
    Imprimatur: Moyses E. Kiley, Archiepiscopus Milwaukiensis

"To St. Joseph, Patron of Silence" is a prayer from *One Small House of Nazareth* by Lamplighter and published by Burns, Oates, & Washbourne, 1935, page 90.
    Nihil Obstat: Ernestus C. Messenger, Censor deputatus
    Imprimatur: Joseph Butt, Vicar General

Illustrations on pages 59, 65, and 95 by Rafaello Busoni were previously published in *Joseph, A Patron Saint Book*, Sheed & Ward, 1958.

More RACE for Heaven Products

RACE for Heaven study guides use the saint biographies of Mary Fabyan Windeatt to teach the Catholic faith to all members of your family. Written with your family's various learning levels in mind, these flexible study guides succeed as stand-alone unit studies or supplements to your regular curriculum. Thirty to sixty minutes per day will allow your family to experience:

- ☑ The spirituality and holy habits of the saints
- ☑ Lively family discussions on important faith topics
- ☑ Increased critical thinking and reading comprehension skills
- ☑ Quality read-aloud time with Catholic "living books"
- ☑ Enhanced knowledge of Catholic doctrine and the Bible
- ☑ History and geography incorporated into saintly literature
- ☑ Writing projects based on secular and Catholic historical events and characters

Purchase these guides individually or in the following grade-level packages. (Grades are determined solely on the length of each book in the series.)

Grades 3-4: *St. Thomas Aquinas, The Story of the "Dumb Ox"; St. Catherine of Siena, The Girl Who Saw Saints in the Sky; Patron Saint of First Communicants, The Story of Blessed Imelda Lambertini;* and *The Miraculous Medal, The Story of Our Lady's Appearances to St. Catherine Labouré*

Grade 5: *St. Rose, First Canonized Saint of the Americas; St. Martin de Porres, The Story of the Little Doctor of Lima, Peru; King David and His Songs, A Story of the Psalms;* and *Blessed Marie of New France, The Story of the First Missionary Sisters in Canada*

Grade 6: *St. Dominic, Preacher of the Rosary and Founder of the Dominicans; St. Benedict, The Story of the Father of the Western Monks; The Children of Fatima and Our Lady's Message to the World;* and *St. John Masias, Marvelous Dominican Gate-keeper of Lima, Peru*

Grade 7: *The Little Flower, The Story of St. Therese of the Child Jesus; St. Hyacinth, The Story of the Apostle of the North; The Curé of Ars, The Story of St. John Vianney, Patron Saint of Parish Priests;* and *St. Louis de Montfort, The Story of Our Lady's Slave*

Grade 8: *Pauline Jaricot, Foundress of the Living Rosary and the Society for the Propagation of Faith; St. Francis Solano, Wonder-Worker of the New World and Apostle of Argentina and Peru; St. Paul the Apostle, The Story of the Apostle to the Gentiles;* and *St. Margaret Mary, Apostle of the Sacred Heart*

The Windeatt Dictionary: Pre-Vatican II Terms and Catholic Words from Mary Fabyan Windeatt's Saint Biographies explains over 450 Catholic terms and expressions used in this popular saint biography series. Indispensable in expanding knowledge and practice of the Catholic faith, this book provides a ready access for the Catholic vocabulary words used in the RACE for Heaven Windeatt study guides. This dictionary also includes a Catholic book report resource that contains suggestions for forty-five Catholic book reports: fourteen writing projects, ten book report activities, and twenty-one topics for saint biographies.

Graced Encounters with Mary Fabyan Windeatt's Saints: 344 Ways to Imitate the Holy Habits of the Saints is a compilation of the "Growing in Holiness" sections of RACE for Heaven's Catholic study guides for the Windeatt saint biography series and presents 344 examples of saintly behavior, one for nearly every chapter in each of these twenty biographies. Enhance your encounter with the saints by practicing the models of devotion, service, penance, prayer, and virtue offered in this guide.

Bedtime Bible Stories for Catholic Children: Loving Jesus through His Word contains twenty discussions of Bible stories that were originally published in serial form in a Catholic children's magazine. Their author stated, "The tales are extremely simple and unadorned. They are real conversations of a real child and her mother." Due to popular demand, the series was later (1910) published as a book, *Bible Stories Told to "Toddles."* The engaging conversational style of this book lends itself well as a bedtime read-aloud that allows Jesus to come alive in the Gospels. The study aids include discussion questions to help foster spiritual conversation, Bible excerpts relevant to the presented story, "Growing in Holiness" suggestions for living the Gospel message in our daily lives, and short catechism lessons for both children and adults.

I Talk with God: The Art of Prayer and Meditation for Catholic Children strives to instill in young Catholics a love of prayer and a practical knowledge of the art of meditation. This prayer book contains prayers to pray out loud (vocal prayer) or in the silence of your heart. It shows how you can talk with God, and more importantly, how you can love God. As you progress through this book—from discovering what prayer is to reading and reciting simple prayers to understanding meditation and then to helps for deeper meditation—you will see that prayer and meditation often go together. Meditation is described by the big *Catechism of the Catholic Church* as nothing more than "prayerful reflection" or *holy thinking*. You can use books, devotions, pictures, holy cards, and images (such as the stained glass windows in church) to help you think about holy people, events, and ideas. Learn how to talk with God each day to increase your love for Him and follow more closely His holy will.

Communion with the Saints: A Family Preparation Program for First Communion and Beyond in the Spirit of St. Therese imitates St. Therese of the Child Jesus and her family who studied and prayed for sixty-nine days in anticipation of Therese's First Holy Communion. Modeling this preparation, the *Communion with the Saints* program will help any family find renewed fervor in the reception of the Eucharist. This resource includes a chapter-by-chapter study of the following four books:

- *The Little Flower, The Story of Saint Therese of the Child Jesus*—to provide the foundation of God's love for us and to encourage a desire for holiness

- *The Children of Fatima and Our Lady's Message to the World*—to show the sinfulness of our world and the need to avoid sin

- *The Patron Saint of First Communicants, The Story of Blessed Imelda Lambertini*—to inspire devotion to the Sacrament of Holy Communion

- *The King of the Golden City* by Mother Mary Loyola—to illustrate Jesus' Presence as a source of grace necessary to live a holy life

Each of the sixty-nine days of preparation includes read-aloud selections with enrichment activities, meditational readings, catechism lessons, and plenty of practical application to promote a growth in holiness and sanctity. Weekend suggestions include a list of over thirty-five family projects. The use of *My First Communion Journal* is encouraged with this program.

More RACE for Heaven Products

My First Communion Journal in Imitation of Saint Therese of the Child Jesus provides a lasting keepsake of a child's First Holy Communion. Saint Therese of the Child Jesus and her family studied and prayed for sixty-nine days prior to Therese's First Holy Communion. This journal imitates that family model of preparation for the reception of the Most Holy Eucharist. Each daily entry contains a stanza of a poem composed by Saint Therese, a quotation from Saint Faustina Kowalska's diary (*Divine Mercy in My Soul*), or a Scripture quotation. Two weekly themes—a floral theme in imitation of Saint Therese and a battle theme molded from the teachings of Saint Paul—are offered with accompanying weekly passages from Scripture suitable for memorization. This journal may be completed in conjunction with the *Communion with the Saints* program or used separately.

The King of the Golden City Study Edition is a new edition of a book that was originally published in 1921. This treasure of a book was written in response to a student's appeal for instructions along with "little stories" to help her prepare for Holy Communion. To fulfill this request, Mother Loyola of the Bar Convent in York, England, wrote a simple story that illustrates Jesus' desire to share an intimate relationship with each one of His children. This new edition contains some updated language but, quite deliberately, does not contain any pictures. Readers, as they progress through this story, will form a mental image of their King, one as unique and personal as their own relationship with Him. The study sections assist with the allegory, connect to the Bible as well as to the catechism, and explore the art of prayer in the spirit of the three Carmelite Doctors of the Church. Although written over ninety years ago for a young child, this book remains a timeless masterpiece of Catholic literature suitable for all ages. (Also available as a study guide only)

The Good Shepherd and His Little Lambs Study Edition is a simply told Catholic tale of four children who meet with their beloved aunt for "First Communion talks." More than a story, it is a First Communion primer that takes the tenets of the catechism and, through naturally-flowing conversations, relates them in the language of little ones to authentic Christian living. As Mrs. Bosch explains, "We might learn the catechism all the way through beautifully, and at the end find ourselves still very stiff and clumsy about loving our Lord. When He comes to us, we don't want to welcome Him into our souls only with answers out of the catechism, do we?" Enriched by appropriate Biblical passages, points of doctrine, and prayers, this story-primer is an enjoyable and effective read-aloud that will prepare the Good Shepherd's little lambs to worthily receive Him in the Holy Eucharist.

A Reconciliation Reader-Retreat: Read-Aloud Lessons, Stories, and Poems for Young Catholics Preparing for Confession provides a basic doctrinal explanation and review of the Sacrament of Reconciliation as well as a Gospel examination of conscience—a seven-day read-aloud formation retreat. To help the lessons come alive and to enable young Catholics to more readily apply these doctrines to their own daily lives, the lessons have been supplemented with pertinent short stories and poems. Each lesson contains reflection questions, a family prayer, and a "Gospel Examination of Conscience" that is formulated according to the dictates of the *Catechism of the Catholic Church*. This reader-retreat will not only enrich and deepen the sacramental experience for each member of your family but it will also provide several tools to help you recommit to leading a virtuous life and to grow together in holiness.

Alternative Book Reports for Catholic Students contains forty-five book report ideas to encourage critical thinking for ages seven to fourteen. These ideas are intended to provoke a reflection on those themes and topics that support and encourage Catholic living as well as some that may conflict with our Faith. Many report topics require an examination of our personal faith life and prompt us to take lessons from the saints to strengthen our own faith in God. The suggested activities vary from written exercises to creative art projects and include twenty-one topics specifically designed for saint biographies. Other activities can be used within a group or family.

Reading the Saints: Lists of Catholic Books for Children Plus Book Collecting Tips for the Home and School Library (formerly entitled *Saintly Resources*) is a valuable tool for Catholic home educators, classroom teachers, and collectors of Catholic juvenile books. *Reading the Saints* will help you discover living books from such popular out-of-print Catholic juvenile series as Catholic Treasury, Vision Books, and American Background Books as well as current series books for young Catholics. Use this book to find:

- Over 800 Catholic books listed by author, series, reading level, century, and geographical location
- More than 275 authors of saint biographies, historical fiction, and poetry written for Catholic juvenile readers
- Publishers of Catholic children's books, present and past
- Helpful advice for collecting and caring for used books

- Hundreds of age-appropriate, accessible living books to enrich your study of the Catholic Church's rich heritage of saints and notable Catholic historical figures
- Information on how to build and maintain your own library of Catholic juvenile books
- Inspiring quotations about book collecting, reading, and the love of books

The Outlaws of Ravenhurst Study Edition contains a classic story of the persecution of Scottish Catholics that was first written in 1923 and was revised and reprinted in 1950. This 2009 edition of Sr. M. Imelda Wallace's *Outlaws of Ravenhurst* contains the revised story of 1950 plus chapter-by-chapter aids to assist readers in assimilating the book's strong Catholic elements into their wn lives. The study section focuses on critical thinking, integration of biblical teachings, and the study of the virtuous life to which Christ calls us as mature Catholics. With its emphasis on virtues (theological and moral plus the gifts and fruits of the Holy Spirit), the spiritual and corporal works of mercy, and the Beatitudes, *Outlaws of Ravenhurst Study Edition* is a fun and effective catechetical tool for Catholics preparing for the Sacrament of Confirmation. (Also available as a study guide only)

The Family that Overtook Christ Study Edition: The Story of the Family of St. Bernard of Clairvaux is an excellent read for young adults who are preparing to receive the Sacrament of Confirmation. In this exciting chronicle of the life of twelfth-century knights, we have an entire family of nine saints who lay before us their individual means of achieving intimate union with Christ. Learn with the Fontaines family how to supernaturalize the natural, develop a God-consciousness, and attain sanctity by being yourself. Perfect for high-school read-aloud (or adult study), this new study edition has over 250 footnotes for increased comprehension and provides discussion/meditation points to promote the art of spiritual conversation. The appendix lists formulas of Catholic doctrine that are essential for confirmands not only to know but also to incorporate into their own spiritual lives.

A Confirmation Reader-Retreat: Read-Aloud Lessons, Stories and Poems for Young Catholics utilizes chapters from two excellent out-of-print Catholic books for children (*I Belong to God, Great Truths in Simple Stories for Children and Lovers of Children* by Lillian Clark; and *Children's Retreats in Preparation for First Confession, First Holy Communion, and Confirmation* by Rev. P.A. Halpin). This book provides a basic doctrinal review of the Sacrament of Confirmation as well as prayer experiences—a nine-day read-aloud retreat/novena. The reprinted material has been supplemented with short stories and poems that provide insights in applying catechetical doctrines to the daily life of young Catholics. Each lesson concludes with "I Talk with God"—a section that encourages readers (of all ages) to deepen their relationship with each of the Three Persons of the Blessed Trinity. Reflection questions promote the habit of spiritual conversation within your family—to encourage family members to discuss holy topics—and to help you grow together in holiness. Additionally, a traditional novena to the Holy Spirit is included.

To Order: Email info@RACEforHeaven.com or place an order from RACEforHeaven.com. Discover, MasterCard, VISA, PayPal, American Express, checks, and money orders are accepted.

www.ingramcontent.com/pod-product-compliance
Lightning Source LLC
LaVergne TN
LVHW011424080426
835512LV00005B/258